RESTROOM RICHES

YOUR GUIDE TO BUILDING A SIX-FIGURE LUXURY BATHROOM RENTAL BUSINESS FOR WEDDINGS, EVENTS, AND FESTIVALS THAT PRINTS MONEY

∾

Nathan Gustafson
The Evergreen Advisor

∾

Elder Publishing

Copyright Information

~

Restroom Riches: Your Guide to Building a Six-Figure Luxury Bathroom Rental Business for Weddings, Events, and Festivals that Prints Money

Copyright © 2025 by Nathan Gustafson

First Edition

ISBN: 978-1-969256-00-4

Publisher: Elder Publishing

Contact: info@elderpublishing.com

Website: https://elderpublishing.com/restroom-riches/

~

Disclaimer

❀ Formatted with Vellum

CONTENTS

INTRODUCTION

Have you ever wondered how a simple toilet mishap could lead to a million-dollar business idea? That's exactly what happened on a sweltering summer day in 2004 when David Sauers Jr., a commercial banker, took his family to an outdoor festival in Savannah, Georgia.

Picture this: You're trying to help your potty-training daughter use a portable toilet while balancing an infant on your hip. The facility has no lights, no toilet paper, no running water, no soap—and definitely no room for three people. What followed was, as Sauers later described, "disaster." Their clothes were soiled, they had to hand the baby to a stranger, and their festival day ended before it really began.

Instead of just going home frustrated, Sauers saw something others missed. He recognized what he called "an untapped market"—the opportunity to create portable restrooms that didn't make people feel like they were compromising their dignity.

That frustrating experience became the foundation for Royal Restrooms, which Sauers co-founded with engineer Robert Glisson. Today, their company operates over 40 locations across the United States, proving that sometimes the best business ideas come from our worst experiences.

Why This Story Matters

This isn't just a feel-good entrepreneurship tale. The portable restroom industry represents a fascinating case study in finding opportunity where others see only necessity. While most people view portable toilets as a temporary inconvenience, smart entrepreneurs have built thriving businesses by focusing on comfort, cleanliness, and customer experience.

The numbers tell the story. According to industry research, the global portable toilet rental market reached approximately $22 billion in 2024 and is projected to grow to $38.4 billion by 2033—a compound annual growth rate of 7.48%. This isn't exactly a "sexy" industry, but it's remarkably stable and profitable.

Who This Book Is For

I wrote this guide for three types of people:

The Practical Entrepreneur: You're looking for a business that serves a real need, has steady demand, and doesn't require you to invent the next iPhone. The portable restroom industry offers exactly that—essential services with proven market demand.

The Local Business Builder: Maybe you want to start something in your community, create local jobs, and build relationships with contractors, event planners, and municipal clients. This business puts you right in the center of your local economy.

The "Why Didn't I Think of That?" Person: You've probably used portable toilets dozens of times and never thought about the business behind them. If you're curious about how everyday services become profitable enterprises, you're in the right place.

What You'll Learn

This book breaks down everything you need to know about starting and growing a portable restroom rental business:

- Market Reality Check: Who actually needs these services and why demand keeps growing
- Money Matters: Real startup costs, revenue potential, and how profitable operators structure their pricing
- Equipment Essentials: From basic units to luxury trailers, plus the vehicles and tools you'll need
- Operational Nuts and Bolts: Route planning, maintenance schedules, and customer service systems that actually work
- Growth Strategies: How to expand from a single truck operation to a regional business

Each chapter includes real examples from successful operators, actual cost breakdowns, and practical worksheets you can use to plan your own venture.

A Word About Dignity

Here's something most business books won't tell you: Success in this industry comes from understanding that you're not just moving waste—you're preserving people's dignity in situations where they have few options.

Whether it's construction workers who need clean facilities to maintain productivity, wedding guests who don't want to compromise on their special day, or festival-goers who just want to enjoy the music without discomfort, your service makes their experience better.

The most successful operators I've interviewed understand this fundamental truth. They don't see themselves as waste management companies; they see themselves as customer experience companies that happen to work in sanitation.

Getting Started

Before we dive into market analysis and business planning, let me share one piece of advice that came up in every conversation with successful operators: Start by thinking like your customers.

Walk through a construction site and notice where workers currently go for breaks. Attend a local outdoor event and observe how people use the facilities. Talk to event planners about their biggest headaches. The best business insights come from paying attention to problems that others accept as "just the way things are."

Throughout this guide, I'll show you how to identify these opportunities in your market, build the systems to serve them profitably, and create a business that grows steadily while serving a genuine need in your community.

Let's begin by understanding exactly who needs portable restroom services and why this demand isn't going anywhere.

1

UNDERSTANDING THE LUXURY RESTROOM MARKET

Ever been to an outdoor wedding where the bride and groom spent $50,000 on flowers, catering, and photography, only to force their guests to use construction-site porta-potties? I have. It's awkward for everyone involved.

The thing is, most people don't even know there's an alternative. When I started researching this industry, I was amazed to discover that luxury restroom trailers exist—and that some entrepreneurs are making serious money renting them to people who never want to compromise on guest comfort.

This chapter is about understanding who actually needs these services and why they're willing to pay 5-10 times more than a basic porta-potty. Because once you understand the market, you'll see opportunities everywhere.

Who Actually Pays for Luxury Restrooms?

Let me tell you about three customers I found during my research:

The Vineyard Wedding Planner

Sarah, an event planner in Northern California, told me about a bride who insisted on spending $800 on restroom trailers for her 150-

person wedding. "She said, 'I'm not having my grandmother use a porta-potty in her formal dress,'" Sarah explained. That one event led to five more bookings from guests who attended.

The Corporate Event Manager

Mike manages outdoor corporate events for a tech company. "When you're hosting potential clients at a golf tournament, you can't have them standing in line for smelly plastic boxes," he said. His company pays $2,500 for luxury trailers at their annual client appreciation day—and considers it essential for maintaining their brand image.

The Film Producer

Jennifer produces independent films and told me actor contracts often specify "luxury bathroom accommodations" for on-location shoots. "We budget $1,200-1,800 per week for restroom trailers because it's cheaper than dealing with unhappy talent," she explained.

Notice something? None of these people started by looking for portable toilets. They all had an event or situation where standard facilities would create problems, and they discovered luxury restroom rentals as the solution.

The Real Numbers Behind the Market

Here's what I learned about actual pricing from talking to rental companies across the country:

Standard porta-potty: $150-300 per weekend

2-stall luxury trailer: $900-1,200 per weekend

4-stall luxury trailer: $1,500-2,500 per weekend

10-stall luxury trailer: $3,500-5,000 per weekend

That's not a typo. A luxury restroom trailer can cost 10 times more than a basic portable toilet. Yet demand keeps growing because the value proposition is so clear when you're dealing with:

- Events where image matters
- Situations where comfort affects the experience

- Circumstances where basic facilities could embarrass the host

What Makes Luxury Restrooms Worth the Premium?

I visited a luxury restroom trailer to see what justifies these prices. Here's what I found inside:

Physical Features:

- Flushing ceramic toilets (not chemical toilet bowls)
- Running water sinks with soap dispensers
- Climate control (air conditioning in summer, heat in winter)
- Interior lighting that actually works
- Mirrors large enough to check your appearance
- Solid flooring instead of plastic grating

The Experience:

- No chemical smell
- Comfortable temperature year-round
- Clean appearance that doesn't embarrass guests
- Space to move around without bumping walls
- Privacy that feels like a real bathroom

But here's what really matters: **these trailers solve dignity problems.**

Nobody wants to tell their wedding guests, "Sorry, but you'll need to use the construction toilet behind the barn." Nobody wants corporate clients thinking, "This company can't even provide decent restrooms." The premium isn't just for features—it's for avoiding embarrassment.

Where the Opportunities Are

During my research, I kept hearing about the same types of events and situations:

Outdoor Weddings

The biggest market by far. Couples are spending $20,000-50,000+ on their weddings and often choose venues without adequate restroom facilities. They need a solution that matches the elegance of their event.

Corporate Events

Companies hosting outdoor client events, product launches, or team building activities. They have budgets and can't risk their brand image with subpar facilities.

Festivals and VIP Areas

Music festivals, wine tastings, and community events often create premium ticket tiers that include "luxury amenities." Better restrooms help justify higher prices.

Film and TV Production

Location shoots often require temporary facilities for cast and crew. Union contracts and talent riders frequently specify restroom quality standards.

Emergency and Long-term Situations

When buildings are under renovation or disaster relief is needed, standard porta-potties won't work for upscale hotels, office buildings, or residential developments that want to maintain their image.

The Psychology of Embarrassment Avoidance

Here's something I noticed: successful operators in this business understand they're not really in the portable toilet industry. They're in the embarrassment prevention business.

Think about it. Using the bathroom is private and personal. If facilities make people feel exposed, uncomfortable, or embarrassed, that emotion sticks with them. They remember the host who put them in that situation.

On the flip side, when restroom facilities surprise people positively—when they're better than expected—hosts get credited for thoughtfulness and attention to detail.

This emotional component is why luxury restroom rentals command premium pricing. You're not just renting toilets; you're buying peace of mind and positive guest experience.

Regional Market Differences

Not every area has the same demand patterns. Here's what I learned about geographic variations:

High-Demand Areas:

- Wine country regions (lots of vineyard weddings)
- Beach and resort destinations
- Urban areas with active corporate event scenes
- Regions with significant film/TV production
- Areas with high income levels and frequent outdoor entertaining

Growing Markets:

- Suburbs with large homes hosting private events
- Rural areas with destination wedding venues
- Industrial regions with outdoor corporate facilities
- College towns with frequent festivals and events

Challenging Markets:

- Areas with harsh winters (seasonal business only)
- Regions with abundant indoor venue options
- Markets dominated by price-conscious customers
- Areas without active event planning industries

Common Misconceptions About This Business

As I researched this industry, I encountered several myths worth dispelling:

Myth 1: "It's a dirty business nobody wants to do"

Reality: Modern luxury restroom rentals are more about hospitality and event services than waste management. Many operators never touch waste—they hire service companies for that.

Myth 2: "Only rich people can afford these services"

Reality: Middle-class families hosting outdoor weddings or graduations are often willing to spend $1,000-1,500 for guest comfort. It's a small percentage of their total event budget.

Myth 3: "Demand is limited and seasonal"

Reality: While weddings peak in certain months, corporate events, film production, and emergency needs provide year-round demand in many markets.

Myth 4: "You need huge upfront investment"

Reality: You can start with one trailer and build from there. Many successful operators began with financing or equipment leasing.

What Success Looks Like

I spoke with several established luxury restroom rental operators to understand what success looks like in this business:

Small Independent Operator (1-3 trailers):

- Annual revenue: $150,000-300,000
- Profit margin: 40-60% after expenses
- Typical customer: Local weddings and small corporate events
- Growth strategy: Word-of-mouth and repeat customers

Regional Business (5-15 trailers):

- Annual revenue: $500,000-1.5 million

- Profit margin: 50-70% after paying for staff and service
- Typical customer: Event planners, venues, corporate accounts
- Growth strategy: Geographic expansion and service diversification

Market Leader (20+ trailers):

- Annual revenue: $2+ million
- Profit margin: 60-80% with scale advantages
- Typical customer: Large events, film production, municipal contracts
- Growth strategy: Market dominance and premium pricing

The common thread? They all started by understanding that this business is about solving problems for people who care more about quality than price.

Getting Started: Market Research Questions

Before jumping into this business, spend time understanding your local market. Here are questions I wish I'd asked earlier:

About Events:

- How many outdoor weddings happen in your area annually?
- What venues lack adequate restroom facilities?
- Who are the active event planners and what do they need?
- Are there recurring festivals or corporate events?

About Competition:

- Who currently provides luxury restroom rentals?
- What are they charging and what's included?
- Where are the service gaps or customer complaints?

- Could you differentiate through better service or features?

About Customers:

- What's the typical budget for events in your area?
- How do potential customers currently solve restroom problems?
- What would convince them to upgrade from basic porta-potties?
- Who influences their purchasing decisions?

The Bottom Line

The luxury restroom rental market exists because there's a genuine need that basic porta-potties can't meet. When people are hosting important events or managing situations where image matters, they'll pay significantly more for facilities that don't embarrass them or their guests.

Success in this business comes from understanding that you're solving emotional and social problems, not just providing functional toilets. You're helping hosts avoid embarrassment, ensuring guest comfort, and maintaining event quality.

The market opportunity is real, the profit margins are attractive, and the barriers to entry are manageable. But like any business, success depends on understanding your customers, delivering consistent quality, and building a reputation for reliability.

In the next chapter, we'll turn this market understanding into a concrete business plan with real numbers, timelines, and actionable steps. Because understanding the opportunity is just the beginning—now we need to figure out how to capture it.

2

CRAFTING A WINNING BUSINESS PLAN

H ere's the reality about business plans: most people write them wrong. They create these perfect, theoretical documents that sound impressive but have nothing to do with actually running a business.

When I first started researching portable restroom businesses, I read dozens of business plans online. They were all the same— generic templates filled with buzzwords about "synergistic market opportunities" and "competitive differentiation strategies." None of them felt real.

The truth is, if you're serious about starting a restroom rental business, you need a plan that's actually useful—one that helps you make decisions, secure funding, and avoid the costly mistakes that kill 50% of new businesses in their first five years.

What Makes a Business Plan Actually Useful?

Let me be blunt: you're not writing this for a business school professor. You're writing it to convince three groups of people that you're not going to lose their money:

- Lenders who want to know you'll pay them back
- Partners who might invest time or money
- Yourself when you're making tough decisions at 2 AM

I've seen too many entrepreneurs get lost in 40-page documents that no one reads. The portable restroom business is straightforward —your plan should be too.

The Financial Reality Check

Your business plan needs to be grounded in realistic numbers, not optimistic projections. Here's what you need to understand upfront:

Startup Investment Range:

- Minimal viable operation: $60,000-$80,000
- Professional setup: $80,000-$120,000
- Premium market entry: $120,000+

Revenue Potential:

- Basic operations: $120,000-$180,000 annually
- Established business: $200,000-$350,000 annually
- Market-leading operation: $400,000+ annually

Key Planning Reality:

The portable restroom business is highly seasonal. Summer months can generate 60-70% of annual revenue, while winter months may barely cover operating costs. Your business plan must account for this cyclical reality—not just project steady monthly growth.

Note: Chapter 4 provides detailed startup costs, operating expenses, and funding strategies. For business planning purposes, use these ranges to validate your concept and assess market opportunity.

Market Research That Actually Matters

Forget about analyzing the "global portable sanitation market." What matters is your local market. Here's what you actually need to research:

Local Construction Activity:

Drive around your area. How many active construction sites do you see? Talk to project managers—they're usually happy to discuss their current restroom providers and what they like or don't like about the service.

Event Venues and Planners:

Contact local wedding venues, especially those with outdoor ceremony options. Many don't have adequate restroom facilities for large events. Event planners are goldmines for referrals if you provide reliable service.

Current Competitors:

Look up existing portable toilet companies in your area. Check their websites, Google reviews, and pricing if available. Don't try to undercut everyone—compete on service quality and reliability.

I found one entrepreneur who spent three months driving around before starting his business. He identified every competitor's trucks, counted units at job sites, and talked to dozens of customers. By the time he opened, he knew exactly where the gaps were.

Strategic Decisions That Shape Everything

You can't serve everyone well, so pick your focus:

The Construction Route:

Pros: Steady, predictable income; long-term contracts; less weekend work

Cons: Lower per-unit pricing; dealing with rough job sites; payment can be slow

The Event Route:

Pros: Higher margins; weekend premium pricing; cleaner work environment

Cons: Seasonal fluctuations; last-minute changes; one-time customers

The Hybrid Approach:

Many successful operators I've researched use construction contracts as their base income, then add events for higher margins. This requires more equipment and logistics but provides steadier cash flow.

Financial Planning Without Fantasy

Your financial projections need to be honest, especially if you're seeking funding. Here's a realistic first-year scenario based on actual industry operators:

Conservative Scenario:

- 15 standard units, 2 luxury units
- 40% average utilization (factoring in seasonal slowdowns)
- Annual revenue: $120,000-$150,000
- Net profit margin: 15-20% (after all expenses including your salary)

Aggressive but Achievable:

- Same equipment but 55% utilization through better marketing
- Annual revenue: $180,000-$220,000
- Net profit margin: 25-30%

The difference between these scenarios usually comes down to how aggressively you pursue contracts and how good you are at customer service. One missed pickup or dirty unit can kill repeat business.

Common Planning Mistakes That Cost Money

Mistake #1: Underestimating Insurance Costs

Commercial liability insurance for portable toilets isn't cheap. Budget at least $8,000 annually for comprehensive coverage. I've seen new operators shocked by insurance quotes that doubled their projected expenses.

Mistake #2: Not Planning for Equipment Replacement

Porta-potties last 7-10 years with proper maintenance, but pumps, hoses, and truck equipment need regular replacement. Set aside 10% of revenue for equipment reserves.

Mistake #3: Ignoring Regulatory Requirements

Every state has different rules for waste disposal, transportation, and health permits. Factor in at least $2,000-$5,000 for initial licensing and permit fees.

Mistake #4: Fantasizing About Growth

Don't plan to add 20 units in year two unless you've identified specific demand. Growth requires additional truck capacity, storage space, and working capital.

Securing Funding: What Actually Works

If you need outside funding, here's what matters to lenders:

Personal Investment: Put your own money in first. Lenders want to see you have skin in the game—typically 20-30% of the total startup cost.

Industry Experience: If you've worked in construction, event planning, or service industries, highlight that. If not, consider working for an existing company part-time to learn the business.

Local Market Research: Specific data about your area impresses lenders more than national industry statistics. Show them you understand your local competition and customer base.

Conservative Projections: Lenders prefer realistic projections over aggressive growth scenarios. They'd rather fund someone who under-promises and over-delivers.

Your Action Plan

Instead of writing a perfect 30-page business plan, start with a focused 5-page summary:

- One-page executive summary with your basic concept and financial highlights
- Local market analysis with specific research about your area
- Startup budget and 3-year projections using real industry numbers
- Marketing strategy focused on your chosen customer segment
- Risk management plan addressing seasonal fluctuations and potential problems

Test your assumptions before you commit. Rent a unit for a weekend and see how the logistics work. Talk to potential customers about their current providers and what they'd want from a new company.

The portable restroom business is straightforward, but it's not easy. Success comes down to reliable service, smart planning, and understanding your local market. Skip the business school jargon and focus on the fundamentals that actually matter.

Key Takeaways

- Budget realistically: Plan for $60,000-$100,000 in startup costs with 6 months of operating expenses
- Pick your focus: Construction contracts for steady income, events for higher margins, or a hybrid approach
- Research locally: National statistics matter less than understanding your specific market

- Plan for seasonality: Summer is busy, winter is slow—your cash flow plan must account for this
- Start conservative: It's easier to grow from a profitable base than to recover from overextension

The businesses that succeed in this industry aren't the ones with the prettiest plans—they're the ones with realistic expectations and relentless focus on customer service.

Next Steps: Chapter 3 will help you choose the specific business model and strategy that fits your market and goals. We'll dive into the operational decisions that will shape your daily business operations.

3

CHOOSING YOUR BUSINESS MODEL
AND STRATEGY

The question seems obvious, but many operators enter the portable restroom business without thoroughly considering their answer. They purchase equipment, acquire customers, and then realize they've accidentally chosen a business model that doesn't match their goals, skills, or market conditions.

Your business model determines everything: what equipment you buy, how you price services, which customers you target, and how much money you can make. Get this decision right, and you'll build a sustainable, profitable business. Get it wrong, and you'll spend years trying to fix fundamental problems.

The Three Main Business Models (And Why Each Works)

Most successful restroom rental businesses follow one of three distinct models. Each serves different market segments and requires different approaches to equipment, operations, and customer service.

Model 1: High-Volume Basic Service

This model focuses on providing standard porta-potties for construction sites, festivals, and large outdoor events. Success depends on scale, efficiency, and operational excellence.

An independent operator in Texas exemplifies this approach. Running 12 units personally while handling all customer service, he has built his reputation around being the operator who "always shows up when promised." His secret isn't the fanciest equipment —it's reliability that keeps construction contractors calling him first.

Model 2: Boutique Luxury Service

This model targets high-end clients like luxury weddings, corporate events, and white-glove service. It requires premium equipment, personal attention, and exceptional customer experience.

A boutique operator in California charges $2,500 per weekend for luxury trailers and does about $200,000 annually with much higher margins. The key is building a strong personal brand and offering a premium experience that customers are willing to pay for.

Model 3: Emergency Response & Government Contracts

This model serves disaster relief, construction emergencies, and municipal contracts. It requires 24/7 availability, substantial equipment reserves, and specialized knowledge.

An operator in Florida runs 80 units and does about $400,000 annually, but his profit margins are thinner because of higher labor and fuel costs. The key is finding a balance between volume and premium service, depending on your market and goals.

The Real Choice You're Making

Here's what nobody tells you upfront: you're not just choosing a business model. You're choosing a lifestyle.

Do you want to personally handle every customer interaction, showing up at weddings to make sure everything's perfect? Or do you want to build systems that run without you, managing drivers and routes from an office?

Are you looking for steady, predictable income from construction contracts? Or do you prefer the higher margins (and seasonal stress) of the event market?

Do you want the independence of building everything from

scratch? Or would you rather pay franchise fees for proven systems and brand recognition?

There's no right answer—only what's right for you. But you need to understand the trade-offs before you commit.

The Independent Route: Build It Your Way

Most operators start independent, and there are solid reasons why. You keep all your profits, make all the decisions, and build something that's uniquely yours.

I met one operator in Texas who's been independent for eight years. He runs 12 units, personally handles all customer service, and has built his reputation around being the guy who "always shows up when he says he will." His annual revenue is around $180,000, and after expenses, he takes home about $65,000. Not bad for working mostly weekends and having total control over his schedule.

But independence has real costs. When his truck broke down last summer, he spent three days scrambling to borrow equipment from a competitor. When he wanted to expand into luxury trailers, he had to research everything from scratch—suppliers, pricing, maintenance requirements. Every business decision falls on his shoulders.

The Independent Reality:

- You keep 100% of profits, but you solve 100% of problems
- Complete control over quality and customer experience
- Slower learning curve—you figure everything out yourself
- Need significant capital reserves for equipment failures
- Your business depends entirely on your personal reputation

The Franchise Path: Proven Systems with a Price

Royal Restrooms has been franchising since 2004, and they've built a solid reputation in the luxury market. Their franchise model gives you access to their brand, training program, operational systems, and ongoing support.

Here's what their franchise package includes: proven trailer designs, supplier relationships, marketing materials, territory protection, and a network of other operators you can learn from. The downside? Initial franchise fees around $45,000, plus ongoing royalties of 6% of gross revenue.

A Royal Restrooms franchisee who has been operating for three years reported a smoother startup experience compared to many independent operators. With proven systems already in place, she launched with ready-made marketing materials, established supplier relationships, and access to a hotline for operational support. However, she also expressed feeling limited by the franchise's requirements, including specific trailer standards, approved suppliers, and mandatory training programs.

The Franchise Reality:

- Faster startup with proven systems, but less flexibility
- Brand recognition helps with marketing, but you pay for it forever
- Built-in support network, but operational constraints
- Territory protection, but expansion limitations
- Lower risk but higher ongoing costs

The Volume Game vs. Boutique Focus

Regardless of whether you go independent or franchise, you still need to decide: Are you building for volume or premium service?

Volume Operations focus on efficiency and scale. Think construction site contracts, municipal events, and standardized service. You might run 50-100 units with a fleet of trucks and drivers. Revenue comes from high utilization rates and operational efficiency. One operator I know in Florida runs 80 units and does about $400,000 annually, but his profit margins are thinner because of higher labor and fuel costs.

Boutique Operations focus on premium service and higher margins. Think luxury weddings, corporate events, and white-glove service. You might run 10-15 high-end units and personally handle every delivery. Revenue comes from premium pricing and exceptional service. A boutique operator in California charges $2,500 per weekend for luxury trailers and does about $200,000 annually with much higher margins.

Both work, but they require different skills, equipment, and mindsets.

What About Niche Specialization?

Some operators find success by dominating a specific niche rather than trying to serve everyone.

ADA Compliance Specialists focus on accessibility requirements for public events and government contracts. It requires specialized equipment and knowledge, but commands premium pricing and has less competition.

Emergency Response Specialists serve disaster relief, construction emergencies, and municipal contracts. Requires 24/7 availability and substantial equipment reserves, but provides steady, year-round income.

Eco-Friendly Leaders focus on solar-powered units and sustainable practices. Appeals to environmentally conscious clients but requires higher upfront investment and market education.

The key with niche specialization is picking something you can genuinely become expert in, not just something that sounds interesting.

Making the Choice: What Actually Matters

After researching dozens of operators, here are the factors that actually matter when choosing your approach:

Your Personal Skills and Preferences:

If you're great with people but hate spreadsheets, boutique

service makes sense. If you love systems and logistics but don't enjoy customer hand-holding, volume operations might fit better.

Your Market Reality:

Rural areas might not support luxury pricing, while urban markets might be oversaturated with basic service. Research what's actually needed in your area, not what you think should work.

Your Financial Situation:

Franchises require more upfront capital but offer faster revenue. Independent operations can start smaller but take longer to scale. Boutique services require fewer units but higher per-unit investment.

Your Risk Tolerance:

Some people sleep better with franchise support systems. Others prefer the flexibility and higher profit potential of independence.

The Pivot Reality

Here's something the business plan templates don't tell you: most successful operators pivot at least once in their first two years.

One operator I know started focused on luxury weddings but discovered that construction contracts provided more predictable income in his area. Another started as a volume operator but realized she preferred the personal relationships and higher margins of boutique service.

The key is starting with a clear initial direction but staying flexible enough to adjust when you learn more about your market and your own preferences.

Common Mistakes That Cost Time and Money

Mistake 1: Trying to Serve Everyone

The "we do everything" approach usually means you do nothing particularly well. Pick a lane and get really good at it before expanding.

Mistake 2: Underestimating Operational Complexity

Every additional unit, service offering, or market segment adds operational complexity. Start simple and add complexity only when you've mastered the basics.

Mistake 3: Ignoring Local Market Reality

National industry statistics don't matter if your local market has different needs. A boutique luxury approach won't work in areas where customers prioritize price over premium service.

Mistake 4: Not Planning for Seasonality

Event-focused businesses face major seasonal swings. Construction-focused businesses provide steadier income. Plan your cash flow and operations accordingly.

Your Strategic Planning Process

Instead of working through elaborate decision frameworks, focus on these practical steps:

Step 1: Research Your Local Market

Drive around and identify competitors. What business models are they using? What gaps do you see? What do potential customers actually complain about with current providers?

Step 2: Assess Your Resources Honestly

How much capital can you invest? What skills do you bring? How much time can you dedicate? What kind of work do you actually enjoy doing?

Step 3: Start with a Clear Focus

Pick one primary market (construction, events, emergency response) and one service level (basic, premium, luxury). Get good at that before expanding.

Step 4: Plan for Evolution

Your initial choice isn't permanent. Set review points at 6 months, 1 year, and 2 years to assess whether your model is working and what adjustments you need to make.

Key Takeaways

- Your business model choice determines your daily experience, not just your profit margins
- Independence offers control and higher profits but requires more problem-solving and capital reserves
- Franchises provide support and proven systems but cost more and limit flexibility
- Volume and boutique approaches both work but require different skills and market conditions
- Niche specialization can reduce competition but requires genuine expertise and sufficient market size
- Most successful operators pivot at least once based on market feedback and personal preferences
- Start focused, plan for evolution, and prioritize what you actually enjoy doing

The portable restroom business offers multiple paths to success. The key is choosing deliberately based on your situation, market, and goals—then executing consistently while remaining open to necessary adjustments.

Next Steps: Chapter 4 will help you create realistic financial projections and funding strategies that bring your chosen business model to life with actual numbers and timelines.

4

FINANCIAL PLANNING AND FUNDING STRATEGIES

L et's talk about the elephant in the room: money.

You can have the perfect business plan and understand your market inside and out, but if you can't fund your startup or manage cash flow properly, you'll join the 50% of small businesses that fail in their first five years.

The portable restroom business is cash-intensive upfront but can be very profitable if you plan correctly. The problem is, most people underestimate either their startup costs or their ongoing expenses, then wonder why they're struggling to make payroll six months later.

This chapter isn't about perfect financial theories. It's about the real numbers you need to know and the practical funding strategies that actually work for portable restroom businesses.

The Real Startup Costs (Stop Kidding Yourself)

Let me give you the actual numbers from multiple industry sources, not the fantasy figures you'll see in some business guides.

According to current industry data, here's what you're really looking at for a basic startup:

Equipment Investment Options:

Basic Porta-Potty Operation:

- Standard porta-potties: $700-$1,500 each (you need 10-20 minimum to start)
- Used vacuum truck: $25,000-$50,000 (new ones cost $75,000-$125,000)
- Basic cleaning equipment and supplies: $5,000-$8,000

Basic operation subtotal: $30,000-$60,000

Luxury Restroom Operation:

- Used luxury restroom trailer (2-3 stalls): $60,000-$120,000
- New luxury restroom trailer (2-3 stalls): $120,000-$200,000
- Premium trailer (4+ stalls): $180,000-$350,000
- Delivery truck (capable of hauling trailers): $40,000-$80,000
- Generator and utility connections: $3,000-$8,000

Luxury operation subtotal: $100,000-$250,000

Ongoing Costs (Both Models):

- Storage rental (monthly): $500-$2,000

One operator in New Jersey estimates his actual startup costs:

- 50 porta-potties at $300 each: $15,000
- Truck and trailer for transport: $30,000
- Website and marketing setup: $300
- Liability insurance (annual): $1,000

Total startup: $46,300

But here's what nobody tells you: these are just the upfront costs.

You also need working capital for your first few months because customers often pay after services, but your expenses start immediately.

Monthly Operating Costs You Can't Ignore:

- Insurance: $500-$800/month
- Fuel and vehicle maintenance: $800-$1,200/month
- Waste disposal fees: $30-$50 per unit per service
- Supplies (chemicals, paper, sanitizer): $200-$400/month
- Storage/yard rental: $500-$2,000/month

Total monthly operating costs: $2,000-$4,500 before you make your first dollar.

Revenue Reality Check

Before you get excited about the profit potential, let's look at realistic revenue numbers.

Current Market Rates (Based on Real Operators):

- Basic porta-potty: $80-$150 per day, $125-$200 per weekend
- Deluxe/flushing units: $150-$375 per weekend
- Luxury restroom trailers: $1,000-$4,500 per weekend
- Monthly construction contracts: $50-$100 per unit per month

Real Example from New Jersey Operator:
With 50 units, assuming modest utilization:

- 20 units rented monthly: $4,000/month
- 10 units for weekend events (4 weekends): $5,000/month
- 10 units for day rentals: $8,000/month
- 10 units idle (reality of the business)

Total monthly revenue: $17,000 ($204,000 annually)

This sounds great until you subtract costs:

- Revenue: $204,000
- Septic disposal fees: $30,000
- All other operating costs: $61,000
- Net profit: $113,000 (before taxes and loan payments)

That's a solid income, but notice it requires 50 units operating at decent utilization rates. Most people start with far fewer units.

How Most People Actually Fund Their Startup

Forget the textbook funding strategies. Here's how real operators actually get started:

Personal Savings + Small Business Loan (Most Common)

Most successful operators I've researched use a combination: personal savings for 20-30% and a small business loan for the rest. This shows lenders you have skin in the game while giving you enough capital to start properly.

One operator got a $40,000 SBA loan with $10,000 personal investment. The SBA loan had better terms than traditional bank financing and was specifically designed for small businesses.

Equipment Financing (Smart for Large Purchases)

Many truck and equipment dealers offer financing. This can be easier to get than business loans because the equipment serves as collateral. Interest rates vary, but you might get 6-12% depending on your credit.

Start Small and Bootstrap (Slower but Lower Risk)

Some operators start with used equipment and personal savings, then reinvest profits to grow. This takes longer but reduces financial risk. One operator started with 5 used units ($3,500) and a used pickup truck ($15,000), then bought additional units as revenue allowed.

Family Money (Complicated but Common)

Family loans or partnerships are common, but get everything in writing. I've seen too many family relationships destroyed by informal business arrangements gone wrong.

What Actually Matters to Lenders

If you're seeking business financing, here's what lenders actually care about:

Your Credit Score and History

Most business loans require personal guarantees, so your personal credit matters more than your business plan. You'll need 650+ for decent terms, 700+ for the best rates.

Collateral and Down Payment

Lenders want to see you have something to lose. Equipment can serve as collateral, but they often want additional security like vehicles or real estate.

Industry Experience

If you've never run a service business, lenders get nervous. Consider working for an existing operator part-time or partnering with someone who has relevant experience.

Market Research, Not Fantasy Projections

Lenders can spot unrealistic projections from a mile away. Show them you understand your local market, competition, and seasonal fluctuations.

Cash Flow Management (The Real Business Killer)

Here's what kills most portable restroom businesses: seasonal cash flow problems.

The Seasonal Reality:

- Summer: 80% of annual revenue (May-September)
- Winter: 20% of annual revenue (October-April)
- Fixed costs: Same year-round

Many operators make good money in summer but can't survive the winter. Plan for this from day one.

Practical Cash Flow Strategies:

Build Winter Reserves

Set aside 30-40% of summer profits for winter operating expenses. Open a separate savings account and don't touch it.

Diversify Revenue Sources

Construction contracts provide steadier year-round income. Emergency response work (disaster relief) can be lucrative but requires 24/7 availability.

Seasonal Pricing

Charge premium rates during peak season (summer weekends). Offer discounts for off-season bookings to maintain some cash flow.

Equipment Maintenance Timing

Do major maintenance and equipment purchases during slow periods when units aren't generating revenue.

Common Financial Mistakes That Cost Money

Mistake 1: Underestimating Working Capital Needs

You need 3-6 months of operating expenses in reserve. Too many operators spend everything on equipment and then can't cover basic expenses during slow periods.

Mistake 2: Not Planning for Equipment Replacement

Porta-potties last 7-10 years, trucks need major maintenance every 100,000 miles. Set aside 10% of revenue for equipment reserves.

Mistake 3: Ignoring Tax Implications

This is a service business with significant equipment depreciation. Work with an accountant who understands your industry to maximize tax benefits.

Mistake 4: Growing Too Fast

Every additional unit adds complexity. Make sure you can service and maintain what you have before expanding.

Alternative Funding Sources Worth Considering

SBA Loans

Small Business Administration loans offer better terms than traditional bank loans. The 7(a) program is designed for businesses like yours. Longer repayment periods and lower down payments.

Equipment Leasing

Instead of buying trucks and units outright, consider leasing. Lower monthly payments preserve working capital, though total cost is higher.

Local Government Grants

Some municipalities offer small business grants, especially for businesses that provide essential services or create local jobs.

Industry-Specific Lenders

Some lenders specialize in service businesses and understand the portable restroom industry better than general banks.

Your Financial Planning Action Plan

Step 1: Calculate Real Startup Costs

Use the industry data above, but research prices in your area. Get actual quotes from equipment dealers and insurance companies.

Step 2: Plan for Seasonality

Create monthly cash flow projections that account for seasonal fluctuations. Plan your worst-case scenario: what if you only hit 50% of projected revenue?

Step 3: Research Funding Options

Start with SBA loan pre-qualification to understand what you might qualify for. Get pre-approval before you start shopping for equipment.

Step 4: Build Financial Reserves

Aim for 6 months of operating expenses in reserve. This sounds like a lot, but it's what separates successful operators from those who struggle.

Step 5: Track Everything from Day One

Use accounting software designed for service businesses. Track revenue per unit, cost per service call, and seasonal patterns from the beginning.

Key Takeaways

- Realistic startup costs: $50,000-$100,000 including working capital
- Monthly operating costs: $2,000-$4,500 before generating revenue
- Seasonal cash flow management is critical - summer profits must sustain winter operations
- Most successful operators combine personal investment with SBA or equipment financing
- Plan for 3-6 months working capital to survive slow periods and unexpected expenses
- Equipment replacement reserves are essential for long-term success

The portable restroom business can be very profitable, but financial planning and adequate capitalization are essential. Start conservatively, plan for seasonality, and don't underestimate the importance of working capital.

Next Steps: Chapter 5 will cover equipment selection and procurement strategies to help you get the best value for your equipment investments.

5

EQUIPMENT SELECTION & PROCUREMENT STRATEGY

"The trailer you choose isn't just equipment—it's going to make or break your business."

Here's the thing nobody tells you about buying your first luxury restroom trailer: you're going to get it wrong. Not completely wrong, hopefully, but you'll definitely look back six months later and think, "If I knew then what I know now..."

I spent weeks researching trailers online, reading spec sheets, and comparing features like I was buying a space shuttle. What I should have been doing was talking to people who actually run these businesses day in and day out. Because here's what the brochures don't tell you: that beautiful cherry wood interior? It's going to get destroyed at construction sites. That fancy sound system? Half your clients will never figure out how to use it.

Let me save you some expensive mistakes.

What You Actually Need vs. What You Think You Need

When I first started researching trailers, I was convinced I needed the absolute best of everything. Premium finishes, every possible amenity, the works. I figured if I was going to charge premium prices, I needed premium equipment.

However, experienced operators understand a different priority system. As one successful Colorado operator explains: "The secret is buying equipment that makes money, not equipment that wins beauty contests." Her eight-year business operates three profitable trailers that prioritize function over showroom appeal.

Here's what actually matters to your clients:

They care about clean. I mean spotless. Your trailer could have gold-plated fixtures, but if there's a weird smell or the mirrors are streaky, you're done.

They care about working systems. The toilet flushes. The lights turn on. The air conditioning works. The fancy sound system? Nice to have, but not a deal-breaker.

They care about space. People in formal wear need room to move around. That's not negotiable.

They don't notice half the stuff you think they notice. I once spent two hours debating counter materials with a dealer. Know how many clients have ever commented on the counters? Zero.

The Real Numbers: What Different Trailers Actually Cost

Let me give you some real numbers, because the websites always say "starting at..." but never tell you what you'll actually pay.

New 2-Station Luxury Trailer (the entry point for most serious operations):

- Range: $95,000-$140,000
- Popular models: Satellite NuLoo 2+1 ($110,000), PolyJohn Heritage Series ($125,000)
- What's included: Basic climate control, decent finishes, standard lighting
- What you'll add: Generator ($8,000), delivery ($2,500), first year insurance ($4,200)
- Real total: $125,000-$155,000

New 3-4 Station Mid-Range (where the money is for most operators):

- Range: $140,000-$190,000
- Popular models: Satellite Industries Royal Restroom 3-station ($165,000)
- Sweet spot for weddings (150-200 guests) and corporate events
- Real total: $175,000-$220,000 with everything

Used Equipment (how smart people often start):

- 3-year-old 2-station: $65,000-$85,000
- 5-year-old 3-station: $80,000-$110,000
- Warning: Inspect everything twice. I've seen people get burned on hidden damage

In Arizona, Jim purchased a used Royal Restrooms trailer for $78,000. Although it required $12,000 in repairs during the first year, he still came out ahead compared to the cost of buying new. In contrast, Lisa in Tennessee chose to buy a brand-new trailer and later expressed regret, saying she wished she had started with a used unit instead. "I was so worried about everything being perfect that I spent $40,000 more than I needed to," she said.

The Features That Actually Matter (And the Ones That Don't)

Must-Have Features:

Separate male/female sections. This isn't optional for most events. Even if you can configure it as unisex, you want the flexibility.

Real air conditioning. Not some wimpy roof-mounted unit. Your clients will be in formal wear in August. They need it cold.

Good lighting. Women need to touch up makeup. Everyone needs to see what they're doing. LED systems are worth the extra cost —they last forever and use less power.

Decent sound insulation. Nobody wants to hear what's happening in the next stall. This matters more than you think.

Easy-clean surfaces. Your cleaning crew will thank you. Hard surfaces, minimal crevices where stuff can hide.

Features You Can Skip (At Least Initially):

Hardwood floors. They look great in photos, but they're a maintenance nightmare. Good vinyl that looks like wood is smarter.

Premium sound systems. Sure, it's nice, but I've never had a client choose my trailer because of the speakers.

Elaborate lighting schemes. Basic LED lighting that works reliably beats fancy fixtures that break.

Marble anything. It's heavy, expensive, and shows every water spot.

New vs. Used: The Decision That Defines Your First Year

This is probably the biggest decision you'll make, and there's no universally right answer. It depends on your situation, your market, and honestly, your personality.

The Case for New:

Marcus in Florida bought new and never regretted it. "I know exactly how everything's been treated. I have full warranties. When something breaks—and it will—I'm covered." He financed $185,000 for a new 4-station trailer and generator package. His payments are $1,850 per month, but he's booking enough high-end weddings to cover it.

The warranty matters more than you think. A new water pump costs $2,400. A control panel replacement is $3,800. When you're starting out and every repair hits your cash flow hard, warranties can save your business.

The Case for Used:

Rebecca in Oregon started with a 6-year-old trailer for $68,000. "I wanted to make sure this business would work before I bet the farm on new equipment." Smart move. She learned the business, built relationships, figured out what features actually mattered to her market. Two years later, she bought new—but by then she knew exactly what she wanted.

The key with used equipment is finding something that's been maintained, not just survived. Look for:

- Complete maintenance records
- Obvious signs of care (clean, organized storage, etc.)
- Previous owner who actually used it for business (not some rich guy's toy)
- Components that still have life left (pumps, generators, major systems)

Financing Reality: What Banks Actually Care About

Here's what nobody tells you: financing a luxury restroom trailer is not like financing a car. Banks see it as specialty equipment for a niche business. Some won't touch it. Others will, but want to see a real business plan.

Equipment financing typically offers:

- 5-7 year terms
- 6-9% interest rates (as of 2024)
- 10-20% down payment requirement
- Personal guarantees (yes, your house is on the line)

I worked with First National Equipment Finance and had a good experience. They understood the business and didn't make me explain why anyone would rent a fancy porta-potty. Some banks just don't get it.

Cash vs. financing calculation:

If you have $150,000 cash, should you finance anyway? Maybe. Equipment financing interest is tax-deductible. Plus, keeping cash for marketing, insurance, and those inevitable first-year surprises often makes sense.

Tom in Nevada put everything on credit to preserve cash. "I

needed money for advertising, uniforms, truck maintenance, all the stuff you don't think about until you need it," he explained. Smart move in his case.

The Dealer Relationship: Choose Carefully, It Matters

Your dealer relationship will outlast your equipment purchase by years. They're your source for parts, service, and eventually trade-in value. Choose someone who'll actually answer the phone when your climate control dies on Saturday morning before a Sunday wedding.

Red flags I've learned to watch for:

- Pushing the most expensive option without understanding your business
- Can't provide local customer references
- Vague about service support and parts availability
- Doesn't stock common replacement parts
- Located more than 3 hours away (for service reasons)

Green flags that matter:

- Shows you similar businesses that have succeeded with their equipment
- Asks detailed questions about your target market
- Discusses long-term relationship, not just this sale
- Has factory-trained service technicians
- Offers realistic delivery and training timeline

Mike at Gulf Coast Trailers in Louisiana is known for going above and beyond. When one customer faced their first major repair, Mike spent two hours on the phone walking them through it—never charging a dime for the consultation. That's the kind of relationship operators value.

What Nobody Tells You About Maintenance

Your beautiful new trailer is going to need constant attention. Not because it's poorly made, but because it's a complex system that gets used hard in challenging environments.

Annual maintenance costs I wish someone had warned me about:

- Generator service: $800-$1,200
- Deep cleaning and detailing: $1,500-$2,500
- Pump maintenance: $600-$900
- General repairs and replacements: $2,000-$4,000
- Insurance: $3,500-$5,500

That's $8,000-$14,000 per year just to keep things running. Build this into your pricing.

Maintenance tasks you'll do constantly:

- Weekly deep cleaning (2-3 hours)
- Monthly generator runs and inspections
- Quarterly pump service and tank cleaning
- Seasonal winterization/dewinterization
- Constant minor repairs and touch-ups

Some operators hire this out. Others do it themselves. I started doing everything myself and gradually outsourced as the business grew. There's no wrong answer, but factor the cost into your projections.

Planning for Growth: The Decisions That Come Back to Haunt You

Your first trailer choice will influence your business for years. Make these decisions with growth in mind, even if you're starting small.

Standardization matters more than you think. If you buy different brands or models, you'll stock different parts, learn different systems, and train staff on multiple setups. Stick with one manufacturer's line if possible.

Consider towing requirements early. A bigger trailer needs a bigger truck. A bigger truck costs more to buy, operate, and maintain. Factor this into your total investment.

Plan storage now. Luxury trailers can't sit outside indefinitely. UV damage, weather damage, and security issues will kill your investment. I didn't plan adequate storage and spent $12,000 on repairs in year two that wouldn't have happened with proper indoor storage.

My Recommendations: What I'd Do If I Started Over

If I were starting this business today, here's exactly what I'd do:

For most markets: Buy a good used 3-station trailer ($85,000-$110,000) from a dealer who provides service support. This gives you the flexibility to serve most events while minimizing initial investment. Use the savings for marketing, storage, and working capital.

In high-end markets (Hamptons, Napa Valley, etc.): Buy new and finance it. Your clients expect perfection and will pay for it. The monthly payment is worth the peace of mind and warranty protection.

In commercial/construction markets: Buy used and built tough. Focus on durability over beauty. These clients care about function and price, not aesthetics.

My specific recommendations:

- First choice: 3-station Satellite Industries trailer (new or 3-4 years old)
- Second choice: PolyJohn Heritage Series
- Avoid initially: Anything with more than 4 stations (too complex for beginners)

Essential add-ons:

- Quality generator sized properly for the trailer
- Professional delivery and setup training
- First-year maintenance agreement
- Comprehensive insurance from day one

The Bottom Line: Equipment Is Important, But It's Not Everything

Here's what I wish someone had told me: the difference between a $95,000 trailer and a $140,000 trailer matters less than the difference between good service and bad service. I've seen operators with basic equipment dominate their markets because they were reliable, clean, and professional.

Your trailer is important. Buy quality, maintain it well, and choose features that matter to your market. But don't let perfect equipment decisions prevent you from starting a good business. You can always upgrade later when you're making money.

The goal is to start generating revenue as quickly as possible while providing a service your clients will recommend to others. Everything else—the fancy finishes, the premium sound systems, the perfect equipment—can come later when you understand your market and have cash flow to support it.

Focus on getting a solid, clean, reliable trailer that serves your target market well. Then get out there and start booking events. The best equipment in the world won't make you money sitting in storage while you perfect every detail.

Next Up: Legal Protection and Compliance

Once you've got your equipment sorted, Chapter 6 will walk you through the legal side of this business—licenses, insurance, contracts, and all the paperwork that keeps you out of trouble. It's not the fun part, but it's the stuff that protects everything you're building.

6

LEGAL FOUNDATION & RISK MANAGEMENT STRATEGY

"Compliance isn't expensive, non-compliance is"

Consider this cautionary scenario: A new business owner feels confident about their startup progress. They have acquired a beautiful trailer, secured several bookings, and feel ready to launch their operation successfully.

Then comes the unexpected phone call from the county health department.

"We understand you're operating a portable sanitation business without the proper permits. We need to discuss this immediately."

This situation illustrates a costly reality: enthusiasm to generate revenue can lead entrepreneurs to skip "minor" legal requirements. What appears to be optional bureaucracy often represents mandatory compliance obligations. Such oversights result in substantial fines, operational shutdowns, and expensive crash courses in business regulations.

Building a solid legal foundation from the start prevents these costly mistakes.

Business Structure: The Foundation That Protects Everything

Business structure decisions may seem like bureaucratic paperwork, but they can determine whether you lose everything you own or maintain protection during legal challenges.

Why an LLC is probably your best bet:

An LLC provides the ideal balance for most luxury restroom businesses:

Your house is safe. When that drunk wedding guest decides to climb on your trailer and breaks his leg, he can sue your business. But he can't touch your personal assets—your house, your car, your savings. That protection alone is worth every penny of setup costs.

Taxes don't kill you. LLCs have "pass-through" taxation, which means the business doesn't pay taxes—you do, on your personal return. No double taxation, no corporate tax returns, just straightforward reporting.

Banks take you seriously. Try getting a business loan as a sole proprietorship. I'll wait. Having an LLC makes you look legitimate to lenders, suppliers, and high-end clients.

You can actually run a business. Unlike corporations, LLCs don't require board meetings, minutes, or complex record-keeping. You can focus on making money instead of paperwork.

The real cost breakdown:

- State filing fees: $50-$500 (varies by state)
- Registered agent service: $150-$300/year
- Operating agreement (lawyer): $500-$1,500
- EIN (free from IRS directly)
- Total first year: $700-$2,300

Some people try to save money by skipping the lawyer for the operating agreement. If you have partners, don't. I've seen partnerships implode over simple disagreements that a good operating agreement would have prevented.

Permits and Licenses: The Stuff You Can't Ignore

This is where things get complicated fast, because every state—and sometimes every county—has different rules. What's legal in Texas might get you shut down in California.

The permits you definitely need:

Business license. Every city or county wants their cut. This is usually straightforward—fill out forms, pay fees, get license. Costs range from $50-$500 depending on location.

Waste hauler permit. This is a big one that can get you in trouble. Most states require special permits to transport sewage. The application process includes:

- Detailed business plan
- Proof of insurance (specific coverage amounts)
- Equipment inspection
- Sometimes a written test on waste handling procedures

In Florida, this took six weeks and $750. In Texas, it was three weeks and $200. Plan accordingly.

DOT number. If your truck and trailer together weigh more than 10,000 pounds (and they probably will), you need a USDOT number. It's free, but there's paperwork and inspections involved.

Commercial driver's license. This one depends on your truck size and your state. Some states require a CDL for any commercial vehicle over 26,000 pounds. Others have different thresholds. Check before you buy your truck—finding out you need a CDL after purchasing a big truck is not fun.

The permits that might surprise you:

Oversize load permits. Many luxury trailers are wider than standard traffic lanes, which can require special permits for transport. One operator found this out the hard way after getting pulled over while hauling a new trailer home. The officer was polite—but the ticket still came.

Local event permits. Some cities require permits for any commercial activity at events, even on private property. A wedding planner in San Antonio told me about a vendor who got kicked out of a reception because they didn't have the right permits.

Special event insurance. Not technically a permit, but many venues require additional insurance coverage for their specific event. This can add $200-$500 per event if you're not prepared.

Insurance: Your Financial Life Jacket

Insurance in this business isn't just about compliance—it's about staying in business when something goes wrong. And something will go wrong. It's not if, it's when.

General liability: The foundation

This covers you when someone gets hurt or something gets damaged because of your business. Minimum coverage should be $1 million per incident, $2 million total.

Cost: $1,200-$2,500 per year depending on your coverage and claims history.

Real example: A client's dog was spooked by generator noise and bit a guest. Even though the incident wasn't directly the operator's fault, their insurance covered the medical bills and legal costs. The total claim came to $8,400. Without insurance, that expense would have been out-of-pocket.

Commercial auto: Protecting your rolling assets

Your personal auto insurance won't cover business use. You need commercial coverage for your truck and trailer.

What it covers:

- Damage to your vehicle and trailer
- Damage you cause to other vehicles
- Theft of equipment
- Cargo coverage (protects client property in your care)

Cost: $3,000-$6,000 per year depending on your vehicle, driving record, and coverage limits.

The coverage most people skip (but shouldn't):

Inland marine insurance. This protects your trailer and equipment when they're not attached to your truck. If someone steals your trailer from a job site or storms damage it while it's deployed, this covers replacement.

Business interruption insurance. If your trailer gets destroyed and you can't work while waiting for a replacement, this covers lost income. When Dave's trailer got totaled in a hailstorm, business interruption insurance paid his bills for six weeks while he waited for a new unit.

Pollution liability. If you spill waste during transport or pumping, this covers cleanup costs and environmental damage claims. It's specialized coverage, but some accidents can cost $50,000+ to clean up.

Professional liability. Covers you if a client claims your advice or service caused them financial harm. Sounds unlikely until a wedding planner sues you claiming your late delivery ruined her reputation.

Finding the right insurance agent:

Don't go to your regular car insurance agent for this. You need someone who understands the portable sanitation industry. I went through three agents before finding one who really understood my business.

Questions to ask potential agents:

- How many portable sanitation clients do you have?
- Can you provide references from similar businesses?
- Do you understand waste hauler insurance requirements?
- What's the claims process if something happens on a weekend?

Good agents will ask you detailed questions about your business model, equipment, and target markets. If they're just trying to sell you a standard package, find someone else.

Contracts: Protecting Yourself in Writing

Your rental agreement isn't just paperwork—it's your first line of defense when things go sideways. And in this business, things go sideways more often than you'd think.

What your contract must include:

Crystal clear responsibilities. Who provides power? Who sets up the unit? What happens if the client moves it? I once had a client move our trailer closer to their venue for "better access." They didn't tell us, we couldn't find it for pickup, and chaos ensued.

Damage policies that actually work. Define normal wear vs. damage that requires payment. Pictures help here. We take photos before and after every rental.

Real example: Client claimed the scratches on the door were there when we delivered. Good thing we had photos proving otherwise. They paid the $650 repair bill without further argument.

Payment terms with teeth. When do they pay? What happens if they're late? Can you remove equipment for non-payment?

I learned this lesson when a client bounced their deposit check the day before a wedding. Our contract allowed us to demand cash before setup. Awkward conversation, but we got paid.

Cancellation policies that protect you. Weather cancellations, last-minute changes, vendor substitutions—spell out who pays what when plans change.

The clauses that save your business:

Hold harmless agreements. This says the client takes responsibility for safe use of your equipment. It won't protect you from everything, but it helps when someone does something stupid.

Access requirements. Specify vehicle access, ground conditions, and setup space. One client failed to mention their venue was down a narrow dirt road that turned into a mud pit when it rained. Our truck got stuck, required a tow, and delayed three other deliveries.

Force majeure (acts of God). Natural disasters, government shutdowns, pandemics—stuff nobody can control. Your contract should address what happens when the impossible occurs.

Getting contracts that actually work:

Spend money on a good lawyer to draft your standard contract. It's not cheap ($1,500-$3,000), but it's cheaper than losing a lawsuit.

Have them customize it for your state's laws. Contract law varies significantly between states, and what works in Texas might be unenforceable in New York.

Update it regularly. Laws change, you learn from experience, and your business evolves. Review your contract annually with your lawyer.

The Real-World Compliance Checklist

Here's what I actually do to stay compliant, based on years of making mistakes so you don't have to:

Weekly tasks:

- Check insurance certificates for upcoming events
- Review any new local ordinances or regulations
- Update driver logs and vehicle inspection records
- Review and file any regulatory correspondence

Monthly tasks:

- Verify all permits are current
- Review and reconcile waste disposal records
- Update employee training records
- Check equipment for compliance with accessibility requirements

Quarterly tasks:

- Insurance policy review and updates
- Contract template review for needed changes
- Employee safety training sessions
- Professional development and industry education

Annual tasks:

- Comprehensive legal and compliance audit
- Insurance carrier shopping and renewal
- Business license and permit renewals
- Professional consultation with lawyer and accountant

The tools that make compliance easier:

Digital record keeping. I use Google Drive to store everything in the cloud. Organized folders for permits, insurance, contracts, and inspection records. Access from anywhere, automatic backup, and easy sharing with accountants or lawyers.

Calendar reminders. Everything important goes in my phone calendar with multiple reminders. Permit renewals, insurance deadlines, required training—if it has a date, it gets a reminder.

Professional relationships. I have a lawyer, accountant, and insurance agent who understand my business. When questions come up, I have experts to call instead of guessing.

What This Actually Costs (The Real Numbers)

Let me give you the real annual costs for proper legal compliance and protection:

Legal structure and maintenance:

- LLC annual fees: $200-$800 (varies by state)
- Registered agent: $200/year
- Legal consultation: $1,000-$2,000/year

Permits and licenses:

- Business licenses: $100-$500/year
- Waste hauler permit: $200-$1,000/year (varies dramatically by state)
- DOT compliance: $500-$1,500/year

Insurance (for one trailer operation):

- General liability: $1,500-$2,500/year
- Commercial auto: $3,000-$6,000/year
- Inland marine: $800-$1,200/year
- Pollution liability: $600-$1,000/year
- Total insurance: $5,900-$10,700/year

Professional services:

- Accounting: $2,000-$4,000/year
- Legal updates: $500-$1,500/year

Grand total: $10,400-$21,200 per year

That sounds like a lot, but it's about 8-12% of gross revenue for most successful operations. And it's way less expensive than getting sued or shut down.

State-by-State Reality Check

Every state is different, and some are much more complicated than others. Here's what I've learned from operators around the country:

Texas: Relatively business-friendly. Straightforward permitting, reasonable fees, minimal bureaucracy.

California: Expensive and complex. Detailed environmental regulations, high permit fees, strict enforcement. Plan on 2-3 times the costs of other states.

Florida: Mixed bag. Varies significantly by county. Some areas are simple, others require extensive paperwork and inspections.

New York: Complex regulations but reasonable enforcement. High costs but predictable requirements.

Before expanding to any new state, connect with local operators or industry associations. The Portable Sanitation Association International (PSAI) has state chapters with experienced members who can guide you through local requirements.

When Things Go Wrong: Damage Control

Despite your best efforts, problems will arise. Here's how to handle them professionally:

Permit violations: Cooperate fully with regulators. Most violations can be resolved with fines and corrective action if you're cooperative and demonstrate good faith efforts to comply.

Insurance claims: Report immediately, even if you're not sure coverage applies. Document everything with photos and written statements. Let your insurance company handle communications with other parties.

Contract disputes: Try to resolve directly with clients first. Most problems come from misunderstandings rather than bad faith. If that doesn't work, consult your lawyer before taking action.

Equipment accidents: Safety first—secure the scene and get medical help if needed. Document everything but don't admit fault. Let your insurance company investigate and handle claims.

Building Credibility Through Compliance

Here's something nobody talks about: proper legal compliance becomes a competitive advantage. When clients see that you have all the right insurance, permits, and professional contracts, they trust you with their important events.

I've won contracts specifically because I could provide current certificates of insurance and detailed compliance documentation. Event planners and corporate clients choose vendors who won't create legal problems for them.

Your legal foundation isn't just protection—it's a sales tool that demonstrates professionalism and reduces client risk. Frame it that way in your marketing, and watch how it differentiates you from operators who cut corners.

The Bottom Line: Do It Right the First Time

Legal compliance isn't the fun part of this business, but it's the foundation everything else is built on. You can have the most beautiful trailer in the world, but if you're not properly protected and compliant, one bad event can end everything.

Start with proper business structure, get the right insurance, understand your permit requirements, and build systems that keep you compliant without consuming all your time. Yes, it costs money. Yes, it takes effort. But it's infinitely cheaper than the alternatives.

I learned these lessons the hard way so you don't have to. Build your business on a solid legal foundation, and operate with the confidence that comes from knowing you're properly protected.

Next Up: Building Your Brand and Marketing Strategy

Now that your legal foundation is solid, Chapter 7 will show you how to leverage that professionalism into a powerful brand that attracts premium clients. We'll turn your compliance and quality systems into marketing advantages that justify higher prices and build lasting customer relationships.

Quick Favor?

You've just learned how to build the foundation of a luxury restroom rental business. Your review helps other entrepreneurs discover this overlooked opportunity.

If this guide is helping you see the opportunity clearly, would you take 30 seconds to leave a quick review on Amazon?

Leave Review on Amazon:

To leave a review, navigate to:
https://elderpublishing.com/rr/restroom-riches

Thank you! Now let's continue building your business..

7

BRAND DEVELOPMENT & STRATEGIC MARKETING

"Your brand is what people say about you when you're not in the room. In this business, they're usually talking about whether you showed up on time and if everything worked perfectly."

Here's the truth about marketing a luxury restroom business: most of your "marketing" happens after you leave the job site. If your trailer was clean, your service was professional, and everything went smoothly, clients will recommend you. If not, well... let's just say bad news travels fast in the event industry.

This lesson came from a vineyard wedding in Sonoma—an elegant event with a $75,000 budget where every detail had to be flawless. The trailer looked great, the setup went smoothly, and everything seemed to go off without a hitch. But then, on Monday morning, the bride's mother called.

"The door handle was sticky, and one of my guests commented on it," she said. "Just wanted you to know."

That tiny detail—a slightly misaligned door handle—ended up in the online review. It wasn't framed as a complaint, just a passing note: "Everything was beautiful, though there was a small issue with the door." But to future clients reading that review, the impression shifted.

What had felt like a flawless event now carried a small blemish. That moment made it clear: in this business, marketing isn't about clever slogans or flashy ads. It's about delivering truly seamless experiences that turn clients into enthusiastic advocates who can't wait to spread the word.

Your Brand Is Your Reputation (And Your Reputation Is Everything)

At the beginning, it was easy to think branding meant a clever name and a sleek logo. Hours went into designing business cards and debating font choices. But while the visuals looked polished on paper, the reality told a different story—arriving at jobs in an old, unmarked truck, wearing whatever was clean that day. The disconnect between the image and the experience was clear, and it quickly became obvious that real branding starts with how you show up, not just how your materials look.

That's when Jennifer entered the picture—owner of the most successful luxury restroom business in Northern California. Her setup looked like it came straight from a five-star resort: spotless truck and trailer, professional graphics, even color-coordinated hoses. "Your brand is everything a client sees," she said. "From the moment you pull up to their venue until the moment you drive away."

She was right. Your brand isn't just your logo—it's:

- How your equipment looks when you arrive
- How you're dressed and how you speak to clients
- How you handle problems when they arise (and they will)
- How promptly you respond to calls and emails
- Whether you do what you say you'll do, when you say you'll do it

What actually builds a strong brand in this business:

Consistency. Every interaction should feel professional and reliable. Client calls at 8 PM with a last-minute question? You answer professionally and helpfully. Equipment needs adjustment during an event? You handle it quietly and efficiently.

Attention to detail. The difference between good service and great service is in the small stuff. Hand towels folded neatly. Floors mopped until they shine. Generator noise kept to absolute minimum.

Following through. If you say you'll call them back in an hour, call back in 45 minutes. If you promise delivery at 2 PM, arrive at 1:50 PM. This business runs on promises, and keeping them builds trust.

The Marketing That Actually Works (Hint: It's Not What You Think)

Many new operators assume they need substantial advertising budgets to compete with established companies. They research radio ads, magazine placements, and billboard opportunities. However, industry analysis reveals that over 80% of successful restroom rental businesses derive their revenue from referrals and repeat clients.

Here's where your marketing dollars actually make a difference:

Your truck and trailer appearance. This is your biggest marketing expense and your most effective advertisement. A clean, professionally wrapped truck with your business name and phone number gets seen by hundreds of people every day.

Cost: $3,000-$5,000 for professional vehicle graphics

Return: Priceless brand credibility and mobile advertising

Professional photography. Good photos are the difference between getting called for estimates and being ignored online. Hire a real photographer who understands how to make your trailers look elegant and inviting.

Cost: $1,500-$3,000 for a professional photo shoot

Return: Photos you'll use for years on your website, social media, and marketing materials

A website that actually works. Not a pretty website—a functional one that makes it easy for people to contact you and understand what you offer.

Essential elements:

- Clear photos of your trailers (interior and exterior)
- Simple contact form that goes directly to your email
- Phone number prominently displayed
- Service area clearly defined
- Basic pricing information (ranges, not exact prices)

Skip the fancy animations and focus on loading fast and looking professional on phones.

Building Relationships That Generate Referrals

The event industry is smaller than you think. Wedding planners, venue managers, and caterers all know each other. Do a great job for one, and word spreads quickly. Mess up for one, and... well, that spreads even faster.

The relationships that actually matter:

Wedding planners. These are your best referral sources because they book multiple events per year and their reputation depends on recommending reliable vendors.

How to build these relationships:

- Attend local wedding industry networking events
- Offer to give educational presentations about restroom planning
- Provide special pricing for their personal events
- Send thank-you notes and small gifts during busy season

Venue owners and managers. They see vendors come and go and know who's reliable. Get on their preferred vendor list, and you'll get steady referrals.

What venues actually care about:

- You show up when you say you will
- You don't damage their property
- You handle problems without involving them
- Your equipment looks appropriate for their venue's style

Other wedding vendors. Photographers, florists, caterers, and musicians work the same events you do. They hear conversations and see how couples react to vendors.

The vendor relationships that pay off:

- Always be professional and helpful during events
- Offer to help with minor issues (extra extension cords, setup assistance)
- Share business cards and contact information freely
- Remember their names and ask about their businesses

The Word-of-Mouth Marketing That Builds Businesses

Janet, who runs a successful operation in Austin, told me something that changed how I think about marketing: "Every event is a marketing opportunity in front of 50-200 potential customers. Your job is to make sure they all leave thinking you're the kind of vendor they'd want at their own event."

She's absolutely right. Here's how to turn every event into marketing gold:

Before the event:

- Confirm all details 48 hours in advance
- Arrive early and set up efficiently
- Dress professionally (polo shirt with your logo, clean pants, closed-toe shoes)
- Introduce yourself to the event planner and key vendors

During the event:

- Stay completely invisible unless there's a problem
- If someone asks about your service, be helpful but brief (this isn't your event)
- Keep business cards handy for genuinely interested inquiries
- Maintain your equipment discreetly throughout the event

After the event:

- Clean up and remove equipment without disrupting the event
- Follow up with a thank-you email to the client within 24 hours
- Ask for a review or testimonial if the event went well
- Note any lessons learned for future events

Digital Marketing That Actually Generates Bookings

Most luxury restroom rental clients start their search online, but they're not looking for fancy websites or clever social media campaigns. They want three things:

1. Evidence that you're legitimate and professional
2. Proof that your equipment is clean and appropriate for their event
3. Easy way to contact you and get information

Website essentials that matter:

Google My Business listing. This is more important than your website for local searches. Keep it updated with:

- Current business hours and contact information
- Recent photos of your equipment
- Responses to all reviews (positive and negative)

- Regular posts about events you've served (with permission)

Simple, fast-loading website. Skip the bells and whistles. Focus on:

- Professional photos of clean equipment
- Clear service area information
- Easy-to-find contact information
- Basic pricing ranges (not exact quotes)
- Client testimonials and photos

Social media that adds value. Don't post just to post. Share content that's actually useful:

- Behind-the-scenes preparation for events
- Educational content about outdoor event planning
- Photos from successful events (with client permission)
- Industry tips and seasonal reminders

The marketing that doesn't work (save your money):
Cold calling. Event planners are busy and get tons of sales calls. They work with vendors they trust, not vendors who interrupt their day.

Trade show booths. Expensive and usually ineffective for service businesses. Your money is better spent on professional photos and vehicle graphics.

Social media advertising. The targeting is too broad for our niche market. Most of your customers will find you through Google search, not Facebook ads.

Print advertising. Wedding magazines and event publications charge a fortune for ads that get ignored. Spend that money on building relationships instead.

Pricing Strategy That Supports Your Brand

Here's what I wish someone had told me about pricing: if you're the cheapest option, clients will assume you're the lowest quality. If you're the most expensive, you better be able to justify it.

Price ranges that work in most markets (2024):
Basic luxury trailer (2-station): $800-$1,200 per day
Mid-range luxury trailer (3-4 station): $1,200-$1,800 per day
High-end luxury trailer (4+ station): $1,800-$2,500 per day
Add-ons that justify higher pricing:

- Generator rental: $150-$250 per day
- Extra service visits: $200-$350 per visit
- Premium amenities: $100-$300 per day
- Holiday/peak season surcharge: 25-50% premium

How to present pricing professionally:
Don't put exact prices on your website. Use ranges and always provide custom quotes. This allows you to:

- Adjust for event complexity and location
- Offer package deals for repeat clients
- Account for seasonal demand fluctuations
- Maintain pricing flexibility for different market segments

Sample pricing conversation: "Our luxury trailers typically range from $1,200-$1,800 for a full day rental, depending on the specific features and services needed for your event. I'd be happy to put together a custom quote based on your specific requirements."

Managing Online Reviews and Reputation

Online reviews can make or break your business. Here's how to get good ones and handle bad ones:

Getting good reviews:

- Ask every satisfied client to leave a review
- Make it easy by sending direct links to Google and Yelp
- Follow up 2-3 days after the event when it's fresh in their mind
- Provide excellent service that makes people want to recommend you

Handling negative reviews:

- Respond quickly and professionally
- Don't get defensive or argue
- Acknowledge the issue and explain how you've addressed it
- Show future clients that you care about customer satisfaction

Real example of good review response:

"Thank you for your feedback about the door handle issue. We've since adjusted all our door mechanisms and added this to our pre-event checklist. We appreciate the opportunity to serve your beautiful wedding and will ensure this doesn't happen again."

Marketing Budget Reality Check

Here's the actual annual marketing spend for a single-trailer operation:

Professional vehicle graphics: $4,000 (one-time, lasts 5-7 years)
Professional photography: $2,500 (every 2-3 years)
Website hosting and maintenance: $1,200/year
Google Ads and local search: $2,400/year
Industry networking and events: $1,500/year
Business cards and materials: $500/year
Total annual marketing budget: About $8,000-$10,000
That's roughly 8-10% of gross revenue for most successful opera-

tions. Some years it's higher (when updating photos or vehicle graphics), some years it's lower.

ROI that actually matters:

- New client acquisition cost: $150-$300 per client
- Average client lifetime value: $2,500-$4,000
- Referral rate from satisfied clients: 30-40%
- Repeat booking rate: 15-25%

Focus your marketing spending on things that directly generate bookings or build relationships. Everything else is probably a waste of money.

Building a Brand That Lasts

The most successful operators I know built their brands around one simple principle: do what you say you're going to do, when you say you're going to do it, at the quality level you promised.

That's not a marketing slogan—it's a business philosophy that turns every client into a potential marketing advocate.

Your brand isn't built through advertising campaigns or clever social media posts. It's built one event at a time, through consistent delivery of professional service that exceeds expectations.

Focus on getting that right, and the marketing takes care of itself. Word of mouth is still the most powerful marketing tool in the event industry, and it's free when you earn it through excellent service.

What Actually Matters: The 80/20 of Marketing Success

After years in this business, here are the marketing activities that generate 80% of your results:

4. Professional appearance (truck, trailer, personal presentation)

5. Flawless service delivery that generates positive word of mouth

6. Strong relationships with event planners and venue managers

7. Online presence that looks legitimate and makes contact easy

8. Consistent follow-up and customer service

Everything else is nice to have but not essential. Get these five things right, and you'll have more business than you can handle.

Next Up: Delivering the Experience That Builds Your Brand

Marketing gets people interested in your service, but operational excellence is what builds lasting business relationships. Chapter 8 will show you exactly how to deliver the flawless experiences that turn one-time clients into lifelong advocates and referral sources.

8

OPERATIONAL EXCELLENCE & SERVICE DELIVERY SYSTEMS

"In this business, you're only as good as your last event. People remember when things go wrong."

Consider this scenario: A beautiful outdoor wedding in Napa Valley with 200 guests and an $85,000 budget. Everything appears perfect—the luxury trailer arrives three hours early, setup proceeds flawlessly, and all systems test perfectly. The trailer looks immaculate with extra amenities and premium touches.

Two hours into the reception, disaster strikes. The wedding planner calls with urgent problems: "Your restroom is out of paper towels, the toilet paper is running low, and there's water on the floor. We need immediate assistance."

The response reveals exactly what went wrong. While not a complete disaster, the situation fell short of the luxury experience promised. Guests complained, the bride's mother expressed frustration, and the vendor appeared incompetent in front of 200 potential customers.

This scenario illustrates a crucial principle: delivering exceptional service isn't about having perfect equipment—it's about maintaining systems that keep everything perfect throughout the entire event.

The Three Pillars of Operational Excellence

Successful operators understand that operational excellence rests on three foundations: preparation, monitoring, and response. Master these elements to avoid service failures and build lasting client relationships.

Most event problems stem from inadequate preparation. Here's what professional operators implement before every event:

Two days before: Full trailer inspection and deep cleaning

- Pump out all tanks and refill with fresh water
- Test all electrical systems (lights, fan, outlets)
- Check all plumbing (flush mechanisms, water pressure, leaks)
- Deep clean all surfaces with commercial cleaners
- Stock with premium supplies (50% more than estimated usage)

Day before: Final check and loading

- Re-clean all surfaces and polish mirrors
- Verify generator fuel and test all systems one more time
- Load extra supplies, tools, and cleaning materials
- Check weather forecast and prepare for conditions
- Confirm delivery time and route with client

Day of: Professional delivery and setup

- Arrive 30 minutes early with professional appearance
- Position trailer for optimal access and drainage
- Level and stabilize properly
- Connect utilities and test everything one final time
- Walk through with client or planner before leaving

This sounds like a lot, but each step prevents problems that cost far more time and reputation to fix later.

The Monitoring That Keeps You Out of Trouble

The difference between good service and great service is what happens after you leave the initial setup. Most operators just drop off their trailers and hope for the best. Smart operators build monitoring into their service.

How to stay ahead of problems:

For events longer than 6 hours: Plan at least one service visit

- Check supply levels and restock if needed
- Clean and sanitize all surfaces
- Empty trash and replace liners
- Address any issues before they become problems
- Check with planner or key vendors about any concerns

For multi-day events: Daily service visits are essential

- Full restocking of all supplies
- Deep cleaning between days
- Equipment inspection and maintenance
- Weather-related adjustments
- Communication with client about any needs

For high-usage events (200+ people): Monitor more frequently

- Service visit every 4-6 hours during peak usage
- Extra supply inventory on hand
- Backup equipment available if needed
- Direct phone contact with event coordinator

Here's what this monitoring actually costs me: about 2-3 hours of additional labor per event, plus fuel and supplies. What it saves me: negative reviews, angry clients, and lost referrals. The math is simple.

The Response System That Saves Events (And Your Reputation)

Problems will happen. Equipment breaks, supplies run low, weather causes issues. What separates professionals from amateurs is how quickly and effectively you respond when things go wrong.

My emergency response system:

For minor issues (low supplies, small maintenance):

- Response time: Within 2 hours during events
- What I carry: Full supply kit, basic tools, cleaning materials
- Communication: Text update to client when resolved

For major issues (equipment failure, power problems):

- Response time: Within 1 hour, no matter what
- What I have ready: Backup trailer or portable units
- Communication: Immediate phone call, followed by text updates

Real examples of problems and solutions:

Problem: Generator died during a wedding reception

Solution: Had backup generator in truck, switched over in 15 minutes

Client reaction: "We didn't even know there was a problem"

Cost: $3,500 backup generator purchase

Value: Saved $85,000 wedding and gained lifelong client

Problem: Pump failure caused backup into trailer

Solution: Immediately deployed portable units, had trailer pumped and sanitized

Client reaction: "Thank you for handling that so quickly and professionally"

Cost: $800 emergency pump service + $200 portable units

Value: Prevented disaster and demonstrated professional crisis management

The Quality Control That Builds Your Reputation

Every trailer should receive the same inspection, regardless of the client or event type. This consistency builds reputation and justifies premium pricing.

Professional quality checklist system:

Cleanliness (40 points total):

- Floors: Clean, dry, no spots or odors (10 points)
- Toilets: Spotless bowl, seat, exterior (10 points)
- Sinks: Clean basin, faucet, no water spots (5 points)
- Mirrors: Streak-free and spotless (5 points)
- Walls/ceiling: Clean, no marks or damage (5 points)
- General: No odors, fresh air freshener (5 points)

Functionality (35 points total):

- Plumbing: All fixtures work, good water pressure (15 points)
- Electrical: All lights, outlets, fan operational (10 points)
- Climate control: Heating/AC working properly (10 points)

Supplies (15 points total):

- Paper products: Fully stocked, premium quality (5 points)
- Soap/sanitizer: Full dispensers, working properly (5 points)
- Towels: Clean, adequate supply (5 points)

Aesthetics (10 points total):

- Overall appearance: Professional, luxury presentation (10 points)

Minimum passing score: 90 points. If it doesn't hit 90, it doesn't go to an event. Period.

This level of attention might seem obsessive, but it delivers measurable results. Operators using systematic quality control report 4.8+ star average ratings across hundreds of reviews, while competitors with inconsistent standards average 4.1 stars. That difference translates directly into bookings and pricing power.

Customer Communication That Actually Works

Most service problems aren't really service problems—they're communication problems. Clients get upset not because something went wrong, but because they didn't know what was happening or when it would be fixed.

Communication system that prevents 90% of client issues:
Before the event:

- Confirmation call 48 hours in advance
- Delivery window text 2 hours before arrival
- Arrival text when approaching venue
- Setup completion call with any important information

During the event:

- Service visit notifications (text before arriving)
- Immediate communication if any issues arise
- Completion updates when service visits are finished
- 24/7 emergency phone availability

After the event:

- Pickup notification and completion confirmation
- Thank-you email within 24 hours
- Review request (if event went well)
- Follow-up call for any issues or concerns

What this communication actually prevents:

"Where are you?" - Delivery window communication eliminates 95% of these calls

"Something's wrong with the restroom" - Service visit monitoring catches issues early

"We can't reach you" - Clear emergency contact prevents panic

"We didn't know you were coming" - Service visit notifications show professionalism

The Technology That Actually Helps (And What Doesn't)

Technology solutions vary widely in value. Some justify their investment, others become expensive distractions. Here's what actually helps operations:

Technology worth buying:

GPS tracking on trailers: $150/month for fleet tracking service

- Know exactly where equipment is at all times
- Theft prevention and recovery assistance
- Route optimization for delivery and pickup
- Customer communication with accurate arrival times

Mobile inspection apps: $50/month for digital checklist system

- Photo documentation of trailer condition
- Automated quality scoring and reporting
- Historical data for maintenance planning
- Professional reports for insurance claims

Scheduling software: $200/month for comprehensive booking system

- Automated confirmations and reminders
- Customer communication integration
- Invoice generation and payment processing

- Availability tracking and conflict prevention

Technology not worth buying (yet):

Advanced IoT sensors: Too expensive and unreliable for most operations

Complex CRM systems: Overkill for small businesses, simpler solutions work better

Automated cleaning systems: Don't exist yet for portable restrooms

AI-powered dispatch: Marketing hype, doesn't add value for local service businesses

Building a Team That Delivers Excellence

Growing your business means trusting other people to deliver the same quality you would. This is terrifying for most operators, but it's essential for scaling beyond a one-person operation.

How to hire and train for excellence:

Essential qualities in team members:

- Reliability (most important quality)
- Attention to detail (can be taught, but baseline awareness required)
- Customer service attitude (willing to help, not just do minimum)
- Physical capability (lifting, cleaning, driving larger vehicles)
- Professional appearance and communication

Effective training program (3 weeks):

- Week 1: Observe all operations, learn quality standards
- Week 2: Perform operations under supervision
- Week 3: Independent work with quality checks

How to maintain quality with employees:

- Random quality inspections with scoring
- Customer feedback tracking by team member
- Bonus payments for excellent customer reviews
- Regular training updates and skill development
- Clear consequences for quality failures

Real costs of building a team:

- Additional insurance: $300-500 per employee per month
- Training time: 40-60 hours per new hire
- Quality control: 2-3 hours per week per employee
- Equipment: Additional tools, uniforms, vehicles

Real benefits:

- Revenue capacity: 3-4x with two-person team
- Customer coverage: Ability to serve multiple events simultaneously
- Emergency backup: Coverage when you're sick or on vacation
- Growth potential: Foundation for serious business expansion

Seasonal Operations and Weather Management

This business is heavily seasonal in most markets, and weather affects everything. Learning to adapt operations for different conditions is crucial for year-round success.

Winter operations reality:

- Heating costs: Additional $100-200 per event
- Winterization requirements: Prevent freeze damage
- Road conditions: Delivery complications and delays

- Reduced demand: 60-70% fewer events
- Equipment storage: Indoor storage prevents damage

Summer operations challenges:

- Cooling costs: High electrical demands
- High demand: Booking conflicts and premium pricing opportunities
- Heat stress: Employee safety and comfort considerations
- Supply challenges: Higher usage rates require more frequent service

Weather contingency planning:

- Backup power systems for critical events
- Indoor storage to prevent weather damage
- Alternative delivery routes for difficult conditions
- Emergency contact lists for weather-related issues
- Insurance coverage for weather-related cancellations

The Real Costs of Operational Excellence

Let me give you the actual numbers for what operational excellence costs me annually:

Quality control systems:

- Additional cleaning time: 1 hour per event × 150 events = $4,500
- Premium supplies: $50 extra per event = $7,500
- Quality inspection tools and systems: $2,000

Monitoring and service:

- Service visit labor: 2 hours per event × 150 events = $9,000
- Additional fuel and vehicle costs: $3,500

- Emergency response capability: $5,000

Technology and systems:

- Scheduling and communication software: $3,600
- GPS tracking and fleet management: $1,800
- Mobile inspection and quality apps: $600

Team development:

- Training and development programs: $4,000
- Additional insurance and benefits: $8,000
- Quality bonuses and incentives: $3,000

Total annual investment in operational excellence: $52,500
That sounds like a lot, but here's what it generates:

- Premium pricing: $200-400 higher per event
- Referral business: 40% of new clients come from referrals
- Repeat customers: 25% annual repeat rate
- Reduced insurance claims and equipment damage
- Higher customer satisfaction and online ratings

The return on investment is typically 3-4x the cost within the first year.

What Actually Matters: The 80/20 of Operations

After years of trying different systems and approaches, here are the operational activities that generate 80% of your customer satisfaction results:

1. Flawless equipment condition at delivery and throughout events
2. Proactive service monitoring that prevents problems

3. Immediate response when issues do arise
4. Professional communication at every touchpoint
5. Consistent quality regardless of event size or customer

Everything else is nice to have but not essential. Focus on these five things, and you'll have customers who become advocates for your business.

Next Up: Scaling Without Sacrificing Quality

Once you've mastered operational excellence with a single trailer, Chapter 9 will show you how to expand your business while maintaining the quality standards that built your reputation. We'll cover fleet growth, team management, and geographic expansion strategies that preserve what makes your service special.

9

SCALING YOUR BUSINESS AND GROWTH STRATEGIES

"Growing too fast is just as dangerous as not growing at all."

A successful two-year operation reached a critical decision point. With consistent bookings, steady revenue, and multiple clients requesting additional units, expansion seemed like the logical next step. The opportunity appeared clear: add more trailers, expand the service radius from 20 to 50 miles, hire employees, and capture new market segments.

However, this aggressive growth strategy created significant challenges. Financial overextension, quality degradation, service failures, and operational chaos resulted from expanding too quickly without proper planning. The lesson proved costly but valuable: growth without planning is an expensive path to business failure.

Understanding when and how to scale properly separates successful operators from those who struggle or fail during expansion attempts.

When You're Actually Ready to Grow (Not When You Think You Are)

Most operators want to expand as soon as they start generating profits. However, premature expansion often leads to failure. Here's how to determine actual readiness for growth:

You're consistently turning away profitable business. Not just busy weekends during peak season—consistent demand that you can't serve with your current capacity. Track this for at least six months before making any expansion decisions.

Successful operators maintain a "lost business log" to record every booking they can't take. Date, event type, potential revenue, and reason they couldn't serve them. When this log shows $50,000+ in lost revenue over six months, it's time to consider expansion.

Your finances can handle the stress. Expansion requires significant upfront investment plus increased ongoing costs. You need:

- 6-12 months of operating expenses in the bank
- Available credit for equipment financing
- Positive cash flow for at least 12 consecutive months
- Personal financial cushion for when things go wrong (and they will)

You have systems that work without you. If your business falls apart when you're sick for three days, you're not ready to grow. You need documented procedures, reliable suppliers, and operational systems that function independently.

Examples of "ready vs. not ready":

Ready: Susan in Oregon had 18 months of strong bookings, $75,000 in the bank, documented procedures for everything, and was turning away 2-3 events per month. Her expansion to a second trailer increased revenue 60% in year one.

Not ready: Mike in Texas had six good months, $15,000 saved, and no documented systems. His expansion nearly bankrupted him when his first season with two trailers was slower than expected.

Fleet Expansion: What Actually Works

Most operators assume they should buy an identical second trailer. That's usually wrong. Smart expansion means filling gaps in your market coverage.

If you started with a mid-size trailer (3-4 stations):

Consider adding a smaller 2-station luxury unit for intimate events or a larger 5+ station unit for big corporate events. This lets you serve different market segments instead of just competing with yourself.

If you started with wedding focus:

Add ADA-compliant units to capture corporate and municipal business. Government contracts and corporate events have different requirements but can provide steady revenue and off-season bookings.

If you serve one geographic area well:

Consider expanding to adjacent markets before adding more capacity in your current area. New markets can be more profitable than saturated local markets.

Effective expansion strategy example:

A successful operator started with a 3-station wedding-focused trailer. For their second unit, they chose a 2-station luxury trailer that could serve intimate events and upscale corporate functions. This provided access to events the first trailer was too large for, without cannibalizing the wedding business.

Year one revenue increase: 75%

Year two revenue increase: 40% (growth continued but at sustainable pace)

Geographic Expansion: The Math That Matters

Expanding your service area sounds easy until you run the numbers. Here's what geographic expansion actually costs:

Additional travel time and fuel:

Serving events 45 minutes away instead of 15 minutes away triples your travel costs and time investment. At $100/hour for your time plus fuel, that's $300+ in additional costs per event.

Reduced responsiveness:

Your competitive advantage is often your ability to respond quickly to problems or last-minute requests. Distance makes this much harder.

Market knowledge:

You won't know the venues, the local vendors, or the market dynamics in new areas. This puts you at a disadvantage against local competitors.

Successful expansion example:

Rather than expanding service radius from 20 miles to 50 miles, one operator focused on becoming dominant in adjacent markets. They partnered with a venue 35 miles away that hosted 40+ events per year. That single relationship generated $85,000 in annual revenue and led to referrals throughout that region.

Unsuccessful expansion example:

Another operator attempted to serve a mountain resort area 60 miles away. The travel time, unfamiliar venues, and limited local knowledge made every event stressful and unprofitable. After six events, they discontinued serving that market.

Smart geographic expansion strategy:

- Identify specific venues or event planners in target areas
- Build relationships before expanding geographically
- Test new markets with temporary arrangements before committing
- Calculate real costs including travel time, not just miles

Building a Team That Doesn't Destroy Your Business

Hiring your first employee is terrifying for most operators. You're used to controlling everything, and suddenly you have to trust someone else with your reputation and equipment.

Here's how to hire and train people who actually help instead of hurt:

What to look for (it's not what you think):

Reliability over experience. I'd rather hire someone who shows up on time every day than someone with restroom experience who's unreliable. You can teach cleaning techniques; you can't teach work ethic.

Customer service attitude. Your employees will interact with clients and event guests. They need to be helpful, professional, and represent your brand well.

Physical capability. This job involves lifting, cleaning, and working in all weather conditions. Make sure candidates understand and can handle the physical demands.

Communication skills. They'll need to follow instructions, report problems, and interact professionally with clients and vendors.

Effective hiring process:

- Phone screening focused on availability and basic communication
- In-person interview including discussion of physical demands
- Reference checks (actually call them)
- Trial period with clear expectations and evaluation criteria

Training that actually works:

Week 1: Shadow me on all events. Learn quality standards, customer interaction protocols, and equipment operation.

Week 2: Handle tasks under supervision. Start with cleaning and setup, progress to client interaction.

Week 3: Independent work with daily check-ins and quality reviews.

Week 4: Full independence with weekly performance reviews.

Real costs of hiring:

- Training time: 40-60 hours at $20/hour = $800-$1,200
- Additional insurance: $300-$500/month
- Payroll taxes and benefits: 20-30% of wages
- Equipment and uniforms: $500-$800
- Mistakes and learning curve: Plan for $2,000-$3,000 in additional costs first year

Real benefits when done right:

- Revenue capacity: Can serve multiple events simultaneously
- Coverage: Business doesn't stop when you're sick or on vacation
- Growth foundation: Essential for scaling beyond owner-operator level
- Quality of life: Ability to take breaks and focus on business development

The Technology That Helps (And What's a Waste of Money)

As you grow, technology becomes essential for managing complexity. But not all technology is worth the investment.

Technology worth buying for growth:

Scheduling software: $200-$400/month for comprehensive systems

- Prevents double bookings and scheduling conflicts
- Automates customer communications
- Tracks equipment utilization and availability
- Generates invoices and tracks payments

GPS fleet tracking: $25-$50 per vehicle per month

- Know where equipment is at all times
- Optimize routes and reduce travel time

- Monitor employee productivity and safety
- Theft prevention and recovery assistance

Mobile inspection apps: $50-$100/month

- Standardize quality control across multiple employees
- Photo documentation for insurance and client issues
- Performance tracking and training identification
- Professional reporting for quality assurance

Technology not worth buying (yet):
Advanced CRM systems: Too complex and expensive for most small operations
IoT sensors: Unreliable and unnecessary for manual monitoring
Custom software development: Use proven solutions, don't build your own
Automated booking systems: Personal service is your competitive advantage

Managing Cash Flow During Growth

Growth is expensive, and cash flow during expansion can be challenging even for profitable businesses. Here's how to manage money during scaling:
The expansion cash crunch:
You'll spend money on equipment, insurance, and setup costs months before seeing return on investment. Plan for 6-12 months of increased expenses before new revenue stabilizes.
Real expansion costs I wish someone had told me about:

- Insurance increases: 30-50% for additional equipment and employees
- Storage costs: Indoor storage for additional equipment
- Maintenance supplies: Parts inventory for multiple units

- Marketing costs: Promoting expanded services and coverage areas
- Working capital: Covering payroll and expenses while waiting for payments

Cash flow management strategies:

- Start expansion during busy season when cash flow is strongest
- Consider equipment leasing to preserve cash
- Negotiate payment terms with suppliers
- Maintain credit lines before you need them
- Track cash flow weekly, not monthly

Financing growth options:
Equipment loans: 5-7 year terms, 6-9% interest rates

- Preserve cash for operations
- Build business credit history
- Tax advantages on interest payments

Equipment leasing: Lower monthly payments, upgrade flexibility

- Less cash down required
- Easier qualification than loans
- End-of-lease options to buy or upgrade

Business lines of credit: Access to cash for working capital

- Pay interest only on money used
- Flexibility for seasonal businesses
- Essential backup for cash flow challenges

Measuring Growth Success (Beyond Just Revenue)

Revenue growth is exciting, but it's not the only metric that matters. Here's what to track to ensure your growth is healthy and sustainable:

Profitability per unit:

Revenue / Number of events served

- Tracks efficiency and pricing power
- Identifies most profitable equipment and markets
- Guides expansion decisions

Customer satisfaction trends:

- Online review averages and volume
- Repeat customer percentages
- Referral rates from existing clients
- Complaint frequency and resolution time

Operational efficiency:

- Setup time per event
- Travel time and costs
- Employee productivity measures
- Equipment utilization rates

Financial health:

- Cash flow consistency
- Debt-to-revenue ratios
- Emergency fund adequacy
- Profit margin sustainability

Essential growth metrics dashboard:

- Monthly revenue per trailer

- Customer satisfaction scores (target: 4.8+ stars)
- Employee productivity (events per employee per week)
- Cash flow (minimum 30-day cushion)
- Profitability (target: 25%+ net margin)

Common Growth Mistakes (And How to Avoid Them)

These mistakes are common among operators attempting rapid growth. Learn from these expensive lessons:

Growing too fast: Adding multiple units or markets simultaneously

Solution: Expand one element at a time—either more equipment OR new markets, not both

Underestimating costs: Focusing on equipment costs while ignoring operational increases

Solution: Budget for all growth costs, not just obvious ones

Inadequate training: Assuming employees will maintain your standards without proper training

Solution: Invest in comprehensive training and ongoing quality control

Cash flow neglect: Not planning for the cash requirements of growth

Solution: Model cash flow scenarios before expanding

Quality compromise: Sacrificing service quality for growth speed

Solution: Maintain quality standards even if it means slower growth

Market over saturation: Adding capacity faster than market demand

Solution: Validate demand before expanding equipment

The Real Timeline for Sustainable Growth

Most operators want to grow immediately. Smart operators understand that sustainable growth takes time. Here's a realistic timeline:

Year 1: Focus on operational excellence and market dominance

Year 2: Begin planning expansion based on proven demand
Year 3: Add first additional unit or market
Year 4: Optimize new capacity and plan next expansion
Year 5+: Continue measured growth based on market conditions
Successful growth timeline example:

- Year 1: 1 trailer, $125,000 revenue
- Year 2: 1 trailer, $165,000 revenue (same equipment, better pricing and utilization)
- Year 3: 2 trailers, $285,000 revenue (second trailer added)
- Year 4: 2 trailers, $340,000 revenue (optimization and market development)
- Year 5: 3 trailers, $475,000 revenue (third trailer in adjacent market)

The key insight: focus on maximizing revenue from existing capacity before adding new capacity. It's always more profitable to optimize what you have than to buy more equipment.

Building for Long-Term Success, Not Just Growth

The goal isn't just to get bigger—it's to build a business that provides value to customers, generates profit for you, and can sustain itself long-term.

Focus on these fundamentals during growth:

- Maintain quality standards that built your reputation
- Preserve the personal relationships that drive referrals
- Build systems that work without constant oversight
- Develop team members who share your commitment to excellence
- Keep financial discipline even when revenue is growing

Growth is exciting, but it's also dangerous. The businesses that last are the ones that grow thoughtfully, maintain their standards, and never forget that reputation takes years to build and seconds to destroy.

Next Up: Advanced Competitive Strategies

Once you've mastered sustainable growth, Chapter 10 will show you advanced strategies for market differentiation and competitive positioning. We'll explore how to build advantages that protect your market position and justify premium pricing even as competition increases.

10

ADVANCED STRATEGIES AND MARKET DIFFERENTIATION

"When everyone else zigs, you better learn how to zag. And zag hard."

A common challenge emerges for established operators after several years of success: new competitors enter the market using identical service models. They copy not just the equipment and services, but marketing approaches, pricing structures, and even visual branding elements. Some newcomers literally replicate websites, using identical color schemes and fonts.

This competitive copying raises a critical question: if multiple operators can offer identical services at lower prices, what creates sustainable competitive advantage?

The answer lies in developing differentiation strategies that competitors cannot easily replicate. While trailers and marketing can be copied, relationships, systems, and innovations require time and expertise to develop effectively.

Building lasting competitive advantages requires strategic thinking beyond basic service delivery.

The Innovation That Actually Differentiates (Not Just Technology)

Most operators think innovation means buying the newest, fanciest equipment. That's not innovation—that's just shopping. Real innovation is solving problems your clients didn't even know they had.

The attendant service that changed everything:

At a high-end wedding in Napa, an operator observed the bride's mother looking stressed. When asked what was wrong, she said, "The restroom is beautiful, but guests keep coming to me asking where supplies are, if it's working properly, whether they should wait for someone else to finish."

This observation sparked an innovative idea: providing an attendant for premium events. Not just someone to clean up, but a professional host who could guide guests, restock supplies, and handle any issues so the event hosts could focus on their celebration.

The service was piloted at three weddings with incredible feedback. Event planners loved it because it eliminated restroom-related interruptions. Clients appreciated that their guests felt VIP treatment. The operator could charge an additional $400-$600 per event for the service.

Within six months, attendant service became a signature offering. Competitors could buy the same trailers, but they couldn't replicate trained attendants or the systems to deploy them effectively.

Other innovations that actually worked:

Event-specific customization: Some operators offer custom interior lighting and decor to match wedding themes. For one autumn wedding, amber LED lighting and fall leaf decorations were installed. The photos were stunning, and the bride's social media post generated five additional bookings.

Emergency backup systems: Successful operators develop protocols where every event gets a backup plan. Primary trailer plus a smaller portable unit hidden nearby, backup generator, emergency supply kit. When a generator failed at a corporate event, backup power was running in 10 minutes. The client was so impressed they signed an annual contract.

Concierge service package: For ultra-high-end events, some operators offer complete restroom concierge service including pre-event site visits, custom setup, on-site management, and post-event breakdown. It costs $1,500-$2,500 depending on complexity, but it's worth it for $100,000+ events where perfection is expected.

The innovation process that works:

1. Listen to client complaints and frustrations (even minor ones)
2. Ask what they wish existed (most won't know until you ask)
3. Pilot solutions with trusted clients before full rollout
4. Perfect the execution before marketing it widely
5. Train your team to deliver consistently

Strategic Partnerships That Actually Generate Business

Partnerships sound great in theory, but most of them fail because they're not structured to provide real value to both parties. Here's how to build alliances that actually drive revenue:

The venue partnership that tripled wedding business:

Instead of trying to get on preferred vendor lists with dozens of venues, one operator focused on building deep relationships with three high-end venues that did 50+ weddings per year each.

The operator offered them something nobody else did: a revenue-sharing partnership. For every booking they referred, they received 10% of the rental fee. More importantly, the operator committed to providing exceptional service that would reflect well on their venue.

The results: those three venues generated $180,000 in annual revenue. They promoted the services actively because they had financial incentive to do so. Their guests received better service, and the venues looked good by association.

The vendor network that built itself:

The same operator approached five complementary vendors (wedding planner, caterer, photographer, florist, DJ) with a proposal: create an exclusive "luxury wedding collective" where they only refer to each other and share a coordinated marketing calendar.

Each vendor contributed $500/month to a shared marketing fund. We did joint booth at wedding shows, shared advertising costs, and created a unified brand around "Sonoma Valley Luxury Wedding Collective."

Result: Referrals from this network increased 400% in 18 months. The shared marketing was more effective than individual efforts, and the exclusive referral arrangement created steady business flow.

Partnership principles that actually work:

Make it profitable for them to refer you. Revenue sharing, referral bonuses, or exclusive perks create real incentive to promote your services.

Provide value they can't get elsewhere. Don't just be another vendor on their list. Be the vendor that makes them look good and solves problems.

Create formal agreements. Handshake deals fall apart when business gets busy. Put expectations, benefits, and responsibilities in writing.

Monitor and maintain actively. Check in regularly, track referral performance, and adjust terms if needed.

Technology That Creates Real Competitive Advantage

Technology isn't about having the newest gadgets—it's about solving problems more efficiently than anyone else.

The customer portal that locked in clients:

Develop simple online portals where event planners can:

- Check real-time availability and book instantly
- Upload event details and special requirements
- Track service status and communicate with the team
- Access photos and documentation post-event

- View service history and upcoming bookings

This portal integrated with the planning software that three major event companies used. Once planners started using it, switching to a competitor meant giving up all this convenience. It created "sticky" relationships that were hard to break.

Development cost: $12,000

Annual maintenance: $2,400

Value: Retained $350,000 in annual business that competitors tried to win away

The monitoring system that prevented disasters:

Install simple sensor systems in their trailers that monitor:

- Supply levels (toilet paper, soap, towels)
- Climate control status
- Water and waste tank levels
- Generator operation and fuel

The system sends alerts to operators' phones when anything needs attention. During events, operators can monitor everything remotely and dispatch service before problems affect guests.

This system has prevented dozens of potential service failures. When the AC stopped working at a July wedding, the operator got an alert and had repair service there before anyone noticed the temperature rising.

Technology that's worth the investment:

- Scheduling software that prevents double bookings ($200/month)
- GPS tracking for theft prevention and route optimization ($50/month per vehicle)
- Digital inspection apps for quality control ($75/month)
- Customer communication automation ($150/month)

Technology that's not worth it (yet):

- AI-powered anything (expensive solutions to non-problems)
- IoT sensors for everything (too complex and unreliable)
- Custom software development (use proven solutions)
- Blockchain or cryptocurrency anything (solving problems that don't exist)

Market Specialization: Becoming the Expert

Instead of trying to serve everyone, focus on becoming the undisputed expert in one specific market segment: luxury outdoor weddings in wine country.

Why specialization works:

You can charge premium prices. When you're the recognized expert, people pay more for your expertise. Wine country wedding specialists charge 40% higher rates than general event pricing.

You build unbreakable relationships. Wedding planners who specialize in wine country events develop personal relationships with specialists. They trust the expertise and provide automatic recommendations.

You understand client needs completely. Specialists understand the specific challenges of outdoor weddings in vineyards: power access, ground conditions, weather considerations, aesthetic requirements. Generalist competitors can't match this depth of knowledge.

You reduce competition. Few operators want to specialize this narrowly, so specialists face less direct competition in their niche.

Effective specialization strategy:

Choose a niche with money. Wine country weddings average $75,000+. It's better to serve 50 high-end events than 200 budget events.

Learn everything about the niche. Study vineyard logistics, wedding traditions, seasonal considerations, and vendor relationships. Become a resource, not just a vendor.

Build exclusive relationships. Top operators develop partnerships with premier wedding planners who specialize in wine country events. These partnerships can generate 80% of bookings.

Market the expertise. Websites, marketing materials, and social media should focus on wine country wedding expertise. Don't try to be everything to everyone.

Results of specialization:

- 40% higher pricing than general market
- 85% repeat and referral business
- 6-month booking lead times
- 95% customer satisfaction scores
- Profitable business with predictable revenue

Creating Barriers That Stop Competitors

The best competitive advantages are the ones competitors can't copy, even if they know exactly what you're doing.

Exclusive venue relationships:

Experienced operators negotiate exclusive portable restroom provider agreements with high-end venues. In exchange for exclusivity, they provide:

- Preferred pricing for venue clients
- Emergency backup service guarantee
- Revenue sharing on direct bookings
- Marketing cooperation and cross-promotion

These venues host 120+ events per year. Competitors can see what operators are doing, but they can't replicate it because the exclusivity agreements prevent it.

Trained team expertise:

Professional operators invest heavily in training their teams on luxury service delivery. Teams learn how to interact professionally with high-end clients, handle problems discreetly, and maintain service standards under pressure.

Competitors can hire away employees, but they can't instantly replicate the training, systems, and culture that make teams effective.

Reputation and trust network:

After years of excellent service, established operators develop relationships that took years to build. Event planners trust them to handle their most important events. Venues recommend them to their clients. Other vendors refer business to them.

New competitors start with zero reputation and have to build these relationships from scratch. Even with good service, this takes years.

Financial staying power:

Well-funded operators maintain significant cash reserves and available credit. When competitors try to win business with low pricing, they can match or beat prices without jeopardizing business operations.

This financial strength allows operators to invest in growth opportunities, weather economic downturns, and respond aggressively to competitive threats.

Competitive Intelligence: Knowing What Everyone Else Is Doing

Smart operators spend time every month monitoring their competition. Not to copy them, but to understand threats and identify opportunities.

What to track about competitors:

- Pricing changes and special offers
- New service announcements
- Equipment additions or upgrades
- Staff changes and new hires
- Customer complaints and negative reviews
- Geographic expansion or new markets

How to gather competitive intelligence:

- Monitor their websites and social media regularly
- Attend industry events where they'll be present
- Talk to mutual vendors and venue partners
- Check their online reviews and customer feedback
- Track their advertising and marketing messages

How to use competitive information:

- Identify service gaps you can fill
- Adjust pricing strategies when needed
- Develop counter-strategies for their initiatives
- Find opportunities to differentiate further
- Plan responses to competitive threats

Responding to competitive pressure:

When competitors cut prices, experienced operators focus on value and service excellence instead of matching prices. When they copy services, operators innovate new offerings. When they try to poach employees, operators improve compensation and working conditions.

The key is to respond strategically, not reactively. Panic responses usually make things worse.

Building Long-Term Competitive Strength

The strongest competitive position comes from building advantages that compound over time and become harder to replicate the longer you're in business.

Focus on these accumulating advantages:

- Reputation and trust relationships that take years to build
- Operational expertise and systems that improve with experience
- Financial strength and resources that grow with success
- Market knowledge and insight that deepens over time

- Team capabilities and culture that develop through training and experience

The goal isn't just to stay ahead of current competitors—it's to build a business that's so strong and differentiated that new competitors think twice before entering your market.

The Reality of Competitive Advantage

Most competitive advantages are temporary. Equipment can be copied, services can be replicated, employees can be hired away. The trick is building multiple overlapping advantages that are hard to copy all at once.

When competitors copied basic service models, market leaders had already moved on to attendant services. When competitors figured out attendant services, they had developed exclusive venue relationships. When competitors tried to break those relationships, they had built financial strength that allowed them to compete on price when necessary.

Stay ahead by innovating constantly, building relationships continuously, and never assuming your current advantages will last forever.

Next Up: Future-Proofing Your Business

Chapter 11 will show you how to anticipate industry changes and position your business for long-term success. We'll explore emerging trends, potential disruptions, and strategies for adapting while maintaining your competitive advantages.

11

FUTURE-PROOFING YOUR BUSINESS AND BUILDING A LONG-TERM ADVANTAGE

"The best time to plant a tree was 20 years ago. The second best time is now."

Consider this scenario: An established operator receives a concerning phone call. A younger competitor has entered their market with brand-new trailers featuring unprecedented technology: solar panels, touchless fixtures, and app-controlled systems. This newcomer charges 30% less while booking events the established operator used to secure automatically.

This situation illustrates an uncomfortable business reality: success can breed complacency. Operators focused solely on daily operations may miss industry evolution happening around them. Competitors don't just copy existing business models—they often leapfrog past them entirely.

The challenge requires a fundamental shift in thinking: from quarterly operational focus to decade-long strategic planning. Future-proofing means building businesses that don't just survive change, but thrive because of it.

The Trends That Will Shape Your Business (Whether You're Ready or Not)

Most operators wait until change hits them in the face before they respond. By then, it's too late to lead—you're just trying to catch up.

The sustainability revolution that's already here:

Three years ago, a venue coordinator called an operator with what seemed like a strange request: "Do you have any solar-powered units?" They didn't, but this prompted attention to the underlying trend.

Research revealed that more venues were adopting "green" requirements for vendors. Insurance companies were offering discounts for eco-friendly operations. Clients were specifically requesting sustainable options. What started as a niche preference was becoming mainstream demand.

An investment of $85,000 in solar-powered trailers and water-conservation systems has generated over $200,000 in additional revenue from clients who specifically chose operators for their environmental commitment.

Technology integration that customers now expect:

The younger generation of event planners expects digital integration the same way they expect running water. They want to book online, track service status in real-time, and communicate through apps, not phone calls.

One operator spent $18,000 developing a customer portal that integrates with popular event planning software. Event planners can see availability, make requests, and track everything without picking up a phone.

Result: Booking efficiency increased 65%, and they now work with three event companies that require their vendors to have digital integration capabilities.

The hygiene standards that aren't going away:

Post-pandemic, cleanliness isn't just expected—it's inspected. Event organizers ask detailed questions about sanitization protocols. Guests notice and comment on cleanliness more than ever.

One operator upgraded all trailers with touchless fixtures, antimicrobial surfaces, and UV sanitization systems. The investment was $45,000, but it allowed them to charge premium rates and win events where hygiene is a top priority.

What to watch for to stay ahead:

Industry publications and conferences: Subscribe to three industry magazines and attend two conferences annually. Investment: $3,500/year. Value: Early awareness of trends and technology.

Competitor monitoring: Track what successful operators in other markets are doing. When the same innovation appears in multiple markets, it's becoming standard.

Client feedback analysis: Survey clients after every event, specifically asking about features they wished they had or problems they encountered.

Technology startup monitoring: Follow portable restroom and event technology startups. They're often developing solutions that will become industry standard in 2-3 years.

Diversification: The Insurance Policy That Pays

Consider an operator whose first four years generated 85% of revenue from weddings. They were essentially running a wedding business that happened to use restroom trailers.

When the economy hit a rough patch, luxury weddings were among the first expenses couples cut. Revenue dropped 40% in six months.

That crisis taught a valuable lesson: specialization creates expertise, but over-specialization creates vulnerability.

The diversification strategy that saved the business:

Emergency response capability: The operator purchased two basic porta-potties and one ADA-compliant unit specifically for emergency contracts. When a flood hit the area, they generated $35,000 in three weeks providing sanitation for relief workers and displaced families.

Construction market entry: hey developed relationships with three general contractors. Construction sites need reliable, long-term restroom service. It's not glamorous, but it's steady revenue that doesn't compete with luxury business.

Corporate event expansion: They targeted corporate retreats, company picnics, and outdoor team-building events. Corporate clients appreciate professional service and pay reliably. This segment now represents 25% of annual revenue.

Government contract pursuit: They became certified as a small business vendor with the county. Government events and emergency contracts provide steady work and prompt payment.

Current revenue breakdown:

- Weddings: 45% (down from 85%)
- Corporate events: 25%
- Construction/long-term: 15%
- Emergency/government: 10%
- Other events: 5%

This diversification means losing one major client or market segment no longer threatens business survival.

The add-on services that compound growth:

Shower trailers: Adding one shower trailer to the fleet serves multi-day events, film shoots, and emergency responses that often need shower facilities. This single addition can increase average booking value by $800-$1,200.

ADA compliance services: Every public event needs ADA-compliant restrooms. By offering these units, operators can bid on larger events and government contracts they couldn't access before.

Emergency backup systems: Guaranteeing backup service within 4 hours for any equipment failure adds $200-$300 per event but eliminates client anxiety about potential problems.

Technology: Invest Smart, Not Just Early

Operators learn expensive lessons about technology adoption. Being first isn't always better than being smart.

Technology investments that paid off:

GPS tracking system ($150/month per vehicle):

- Prevents theft (recovered one stolen trailer worth $85,000)
- Optimizes routing (saves 4-6 hours per week in drive time)
- Provides proof of service delivery for insurance claims
- Total ROI: 400% annually

Customer portal development ($18,000 initial, $200/month maintenance):

- Reduced booking calls by 70%
- Eliminated double-booking errors
- Integrated with major event planning software
- Enabled 24/7 booking capability
- Total ROI: 300% in first year

Digital inspection system ($75/month):

- Eliminated paper checklists and human error
- Photos document unit condition before/after events
- Automatic maintenance reminders prevent equipment failure
- Insurance discounts for documented inspection protocols
- Total ROI: 250% annually

Technology investments to regret:

Comprehensive IoT sensors ($25,000): Too complex, unreliable connectivity, solved problems that didn't exist. Removed after 18 months.

Custom scheduling software ($35,000): Off-the-shelf solutions worked better for less money. Lesson learned: buy proven solutions, don't build custom unless absolutely necessary.

Smart everything fixtures ($15,000): Fancy technology that breaks in portable environments. Clients care more about cleanliness than gadgets.

Technology evaluation framework:

1. Does it solve a real problem you currently have? (Not a problem you might have someday)
2. Is the technology proven and reliable? (Let someone else beta test)
3. Can you measure the ROI clearly? (Time saved, costs reduced, revenue increased)
4. Is it simple enough for your team to use consistently? (Complexity kills adoption)
5. Can you start small and scale up? (Pilot before full investment)

Building Systems That Work Without You

The real test of a business isn't how well it runs when you're managing every detail—it's how well it runs when you're not there.

The delegation crisis that teaches everything:

Consider this scenario: A business owner takes their first real vacation in three years, promising to disconnect completely from business operations.

On day three, their phone explodes with calls. A generator has failed at a high-profile wedding. The employee doesn't know the backup protocol. The client is furious. The wedding planner is threatening to never use the service again.

The "vacation" is spent on the phone managing a crisis that could have been prevented with better systems.

This experience illustrates the need for "vacation-proof systems"—procedures so clear and complete that the business runs smoothly even when the owner is unreachable.

Systems that enable independence:

Emergency response protocols: Written procedures for every possible equipment failure, with step-by-step solutions and vendor contact information. Teams can handle 90% of problems without calling the owner.

Quality control checklists: Every process documented with pass/fail criteria. Setup, breakdown, cleaning, maintenance—nothing happens without following the checklist and documenting completion.

Client communication templates: Standard responses for common situations, pricing questions, and problem resolution. Consistent professional communication regardless of who's handling the interaction.

Financial management automation: Automated invoicing, payment processing, and expense tracking. Financial reports generated automatically. Owners can see business performance in real-time from anywhere.

Training and development programs: New employees follow a structured 4-week training program with measurable competency requirements. Nobody works alone until they've demonstrated proficiency.

The management structure that scales:

Operations manager: Handles day-to-day scheduling, coordination, and problem-solving. Frees the owner to focus on strategy and growth.

Lead technician: Responsible for equipment maintenance, quality control, and training new team members. Ensures consistent service delivery.

Customer service coordinator: Manages client communications, scheduling changes, and special requests. Maintains relationships and handles routine inquiries.

This structure means the business operates effectively even when I'm focused on long-term planning or completely away.

Succession Planning: The Exit Strategy You Hope to Never Need

Nobody wants to think about leaving their business, but every smart business owner plans for it anyway.

The conversation that changed perspective:

Consider the story of a business owner who'd built a successful operation over 20 years. He'd never planned for succession because he "wasn't ready to retire." Then he had a heart attack at 52.

His family had to sell the business in a rushed sale for 60% of its value because he was the only person who understood how everything worked. Twenty years of building, and his family got a fraction of what it was worth.

That conversation motivated building succession planning into business strategy, whether it's ever used or not.

Building transferable value:

Documented processes: Every aspect of the business is documented so thoroughly that someone could run it following the manuals. This isn't just about procedures—it's about decision-making frameworks and client relationship management.

Financial transparency: Clean books, documented profitability, and clear cost structures make the business valuable and trustworthy to potential buyers.

Management team development: Strong managers who can operate independently increase business value and reduce dependence on the owner.

Brand strength: A business with strong reputation and client loyalty has more value than one dependent on the owner's personal relationships.

System-dependent operations: Processes that work consistently regardless of who executes them are more valuable than personality-dependent operations.

Succession options to consider:

Family transition: Training family members to take over operations gradually. Requires interest and aptitude from family, plus careful transition planning.

Employee buyout: Key employees purchase the business over time through profit-sharing or installment agreements. Maintains company culture and relationships.

Strategic sale: Selling to a larger operator or competitor who can integrate operations and scale efficiently. Often provides highest financial return.

Gradual exit: Reducing involvement while maintaining ownership percentage, transitioning to passive investor role over time.

Legacy planning: Establishing the business as a long-term family asset, possibly with professional management while maintaining ownership.

Each option requires different preparation and has different advantages. The key is building a business valuable enough that you have choices.

Long-Term Competitive Advantage: The Moat That Protects Your Castle

The best competitive advantages are the ones that get stronger over time and become harder for competitors to replicate.

Reputation compound interest:

Every perfect event, every solved problem, every exceeded expectation adds to reputation. After years of operation, reputation brings business that competitors can't compete for because clients trust based on past performance.

New operators start with zero reputation and have to build trust one event at a time. That's a competition established operators have already won.

Relationship network effects:

The longer operators stay in business, the more event planners, venue coordinators, and vendors know and trust them. These relationships refer business, provide market intelligence, and create partnerships that benefit everyone.

Competitors can copy equipment and pricing, but they can't instantly replicate relationships built over years of excellent service.

System and process advantages:

Operational systems improve continuously based on experience. Every challenge faced has been solved and documented. This institutional knowledge makes established operators more efficient and reliable than competitors who haven't encountered and solved these problems yet.

Financial strength accumulation:

Years of profitability provide financial resources that new competitors don't have. Established operators can invest in new equipment, weather economic downturns, and respond to competitive threats without jeopardizing business operations.

Market position reinforcement:

Success attracts more success. Being known as the premium provider brings opportunities to serve high-profile events, which generates publicity, which attracts more premium clients.

The innovation cycle that stays ahead:

Allocating 15% of profits annually to innovation and improvement —new equipment, technology upgrades, service enhancements, or market expansion—ensures continuous evolution faster than the market.

Competitors often try to copy last year's innovations while market leaders develop next year's advantages.

The Reality Check: What Future-Proofing Actually Costs

Building a future-proof business requires investment. Here's what successful operators have spent and what it's returned:

Technology investments: $85,000 over 5 years

- GPS tracking, customer portal, digital systems
- ROI: $240,000 in improved efficiency and retained business

Equipment diversification: $125,000 over 3 years

- Solar trailers, ADA units, shower trailer
- ROI: $320,000 in new market access and premium pricing

System development: $35,000 over 2 years

- Process documentation, training programs, management structure
- ROI: $180,000 in operational efficiency and reduced owner dependence

Market expansion: $40,000 over 4 years

- Certifications, relationship building, new market development
- ROI: $200,000 in diversified revenue streams

Total investment: $285,000
Total measurable ROI: $940,000
Unmeasurable benefits: Risk reduction, competitive protection, business sustainability

The investment has paid for itself multiple times over, but more importantly, it's created a business that will thrive regardless of market changes.

Your Future-Proofing Action Plan

Based on years of building and rebuilding businesses for long-term success:

Year 1 priorities:

1. **Document everything** - processes, procedures, client relationships
2. **Diversify revenue** - add one new market segment
3. **Invest in core technology** - GPS tracking, digital booking system

4. Build management capability - develop one key employee into leadership

Year 2-3 priorities:

1. **Equipment diversification** - add capabilities that expand market access

2. **System automation** - reduce owner dependence on daily operations

3. **Financial strength** - build reserves and investment capacity

4. **Market expansion** - geographic or service line growth

Year 4-5 priorities:

1. **Innovation leadership** - be first to market with new technologies

2. **Succession planning** - develop exit strategies and value maximization

3. **Legacy building** - establish market leadership and industry reputation

4. **Continuous adaptation** - maintain flexibility for unknown changes

The businesses that survive and thrive are the ones that evolve continuously while maintaining their core strengths.

What's Next: The Conclusion

You now have the complete roadmap for building and running a profitable luxury portable restroom rental business. From initial planning through long-term sustainability, you understand what it takes to succeed in this industry.

The final chapter will tie everything together and help you take the first concrete steps toward turning this knowledge into action.

Did This Guide Help You?

Congratulations! You now have everything you need to build a successful luxury restroom rental business. You discovered an overlooked opportunity that most entrepreneurs will never find.

One Last Favor

If this guide provided real value for your entrepreneurial journey, would you share your experience with other aspiring business builders?

Your honest review takes 2 minutes but helps other entrepreneurs for years.

Share Your Experience on Amazon:

To leave a review, navigate to:
https://elderpublishing.com/rr/restroom-riches

12

CONCLUSION: YOUR JOURNEY FROM
VISION TO SUCCESS

*"You don't have to be great to get started, but you have to get started to be
great."*

Picture this scenario: traffic stops near a vineyard wedding, revealing a bride lifting her gown to navigate around a basic porta-potty. Her beautiful dress risks damage, guests express dissatisfaction, and the venue appears embarrassed by the inadequate facilities.

This common situation represents thousands of opportunities where luxury restroom services could transform experiences and generate substantial revenue. Observant entrepreneurs recognize these moments as business opportunities rather than temporary inconveniences.

Successful businesses often emerge from identifying better solutions to everyday problems. The luxury portable restroom industry exemplifies this principle: addressing real needs with practical solutions that customers willingly pay premium prices to obtain.

If you've read this far, you're likely experiencing your own "there has to be a better way" realization. Perhaps you're seeking independence from traditional employment, looking for business opportunities that don't require advanced degrees or massive capital investments, or ready to build something truly your own.

The luxury portable restroom business isn't glamorous, but it's profitable, essential, and surprisingly rewarding. This journey offers specific benefits for entrepreneurs willing to take the first step.

What This Business Really Gives You

Forget the business school talk about "value propositions" and "market segments." Here's what actually matters:

Financial freedom that compounds over time.

Successful operators report dramatic income growth as they develop systems, relationships, and reputation. First-year profits of $35,000 can grow to $285,000 by year five and $425,000 by year eight, while reducing required work hours from constant availability to 30 hours per week.

Work you can actually be proud of.

Operators regularly receive thank-you notes from brides, event planners, and venue owners. They made their special day better. They solved problems clients didn't even know they had. That kind of direct, immediate gratitude never gets old.

A business that can't be outsourced or automated.

Technology might change how we track inventory or communicate with customers, but someone still needs to deliver, set up, and service these units. This is real, physical work that creates real value for real people.

Recession-resistant revenue streams.

People get married during recessions. Companies still hold events. Disasters still happen and require emergency sanitation. This isn't a luxury that disappears when the economy gets tough—it's a necessity that becomes more important during difficult times.

Geographic flexibility.

Once you understand the business model, you can replicate it anywhere people hold outdoor events. Operators have moved to different states and rebuilt successful businesses using the same principles.

The Mistakes That Will Kill Your Business (And How to Avoid Them)

Many people attempt to enter this business. Most fail, but not for the reasons you'd expect. Here are the mistakes that destroy otherwise smart entrepreneurs:

Thinking bigger is always better.

The guy who bought six trailers in his first year went bankrupt within 18 months. He couldn't afford to properly maintain them, couldn't manage the complexity, and ended up providing terrible service that destroyed his reputation. Start with one quality unit and grow systematically.

Competing on price instead of value.

The operator who tried to undercut everyone else's pricing lasted two years before giving up. She attracted price-sensitive customers who demanded constant discounts, complained about everything, and never referred new business. Premium pricing attracts better customers and creates sustainable profits.

Ignoring the relationship side of the business.

This isn't just about equipment and logistics—it's about relationships with event planners, venue coordinators, and other vendors. The operators who succeed invest heavily in building genuine professional relationships. The ones who fail treat it like a pure transaction business.

Underestimating the importance of systems.

Your business will only grow as large as your systems allow. If everything depends on you remembering things, making phone calls, and being personally involved in every decision, you'll never be able to scale beyond a one-person operation.

Getting distracted by shiny objects.

Every year, there's a new technology, a new trend, or a new "opportunity" that promises to revolutionize the business. Successful operators focus on fundamentals: quality equipment, excellent service, strong relationships, and systematic growth. The operators who fail chase every new idea without mastering the basics.

What Success Actually Looks Like

Hollywood doesn't make movies about portable restroom rental entrepreneurs, so let me paint you a realistic picture of what success looks like in this business:

Year 1: You're working hard, learning constantly, and making modest profits. You complete 40-60 events and generate $75,000-$125,000 in revenue with 25-35% profit margins. You're building relationships and establishing systems.

Year 3: You have steady business from repeat customers and referrals. You complete 80-120 events and generate $180,000-$275,000 in revenue with 35-45% profit margins. You've hired help and created basic systems that reduce your personal involvement.

Year 5: You're selective about which events you accept. You complete 100-150 premium events and generate $350,000-$500,000 in revenue with 45-55% profit margins. Your business runs largely without your daily involvement.

Year 8+: You're the recognized market leader. You can choose your events, set premium pricing, and work as much or as little as you want. You're generating $500,000+ annually while working fewer hours than you did in corporate jobs.

This trajectory isn't guaranteed, but it's realistic for operators who follow the principles in this book and consistently execute over time.

The Decision You're Really Making

Choosing to start this business isn't just about portable restrooms— it's about choosing a different path for your life.

You're choosing independence over security, ownership over employment, and the possibility of significant financial rewards over the certainty of a paycheck.

You're choosing to solve real problems for grateful customers instead of shuffling papers or attending meaningless meetings.

You're choosing to build something that's genuinely yours instead of making someone else wealthy.

You're choosing to take responsibility for your own success instead of hoping someone else will promote you or give you a raise.

These choices aren't for everyone. If you need guaranteed income, predictable schedules, and someone else making all the difficult decisions, stay in your current job. There's nothing wrong with that choice.

But if you're ready to bet on yourself, work harder in the short term for freedom in the long term, and build something that could change your family's financial future, this business offers a proven path forward.

Your First Step (The Only One That Actually Matters)

I can give you 47 different action items and a detailed implementation timeline, but none of it matters unless you take the first real step.

Here's what that step actually looks like:

Drive to three luxury wedding venues in your area this weekend. Park in their lot and watch how events are set up. Look at the existing restroom facilities. Talk to the venue coordinator if possible. Ask if they'd be interested in hearing about luxury portable restroom options.

That's it. No business plan, no market research, no analysis paralysis. Just go look at the actual market with your own eyes and talk to actual potential customers.

If you can't do that simple task, you're not ready to start a business. If you can do it and it feels exciting rather than terrifying, you might have found your next career.

Most people will read this book, feel inspired for a week, then find excuses why "now isn't the right time." They'll wait for perfect conditions that never come.

The people who succeed take imperfect action with incomplete information. They learn by doing, not by reading more books or taking more courses.

What Everyone Should Know

Here's what experienced operators wish they had known before starting:

Trust your instincts about people. The customers, vendors, and employees who seem difficult during initial interactions will be difficult forever. Work with people you genuinely like and who share your values.

Invest in quality from the beginning. Buying cheap equipment, hiring cheap help, or cutting corners on insurance costs more in the long run than doing it right the first time.

Document everything as you learn it. The systems that seem obvious to you after doing them 50 times won't be obvious to your employees or your future self. Write down procedures while you're developing them.

Charge more than you think you should. Premium customers are easier to work with, pay their bills promptly, and refer other premium customers. Budget customers are exhausting and rarely profitable.

Plan for growth before you need it. The busiest times in your business are the worst times to develop new systems or hire new people. Build capacity before you need it.

Take care of your health and relationships. This business can consume your life if you let it. Set boundaries, take vacations, and remember why you started—freedom, not just money.

The Industry Needs You

The portable sanitation industry has been dominated by companies that treat it as a commodity business focused on the lowest cost and highest volume. They provide adequate service for construction sites and basic events.

But there's a growing market of customers who want something better. Event planners who care about guest experience. Venue owners who want their facilities to enhance rather than detract from special occasions. Corporate clients who want their events to reflect their values and standards.

These customers are willing to pay premium prices for premium service, but they can't find enough providers who understand their needs and consistently deliver quality.

That's where you come in.

You have the opportunity to enter an industry that needs upgrading and serve customers who are hungry for better options. You can build a business that treats luxury portable restrooms as an enhancement to special occasions rather than a necessary evil.

The market is waiting. The customers are ready. The only question is whether you're ready to serve them.

Your Success Is Already Waiting

Picture this: a Thursday afternoon while a successful business runs itself. The operations manager handles daily deliveries. The customer service coordinator books next month's events. The maintenance team prepares equipment for weekend weddings.

This isn't revolutionary. It's taking an existing industry, applying quality standards and customer service principles, and focusing on an underserved market segment.

You can do the same thing in your market. The principles are the same, the opportunity exists, and the customers are waiting.

The only variable is you.

The question isn't whether the opportunity is real—it is.

The question isn't whether the business model works—it does.

The question isn't whether you have enough information to get started—you do.

The question is whether you're ready to stop thinking about change and start creating it.

Your success story is waiting to be written. The first chapter starts when you close this book and take action.

What happens next is entirely up to you.

APPENDICES: YOUR OPERATOR'S TOOLKIT

You've just completed an immersive journey through every facet of launching and scaling a luxury restroom trailer rental business. Now, it's time to take what you've learned and bring it to life. This appendix is your bridge between strategy and execution—a practical field manual to help you apply the insights from the chapters into real-world, repeatable actions.

Whether you're cleaning a trailer before a VIP wedding or onboarding a new employee for your growing fleet, the checklists here will help you standardize quality, maintain consistency, and scale with confidence. Think of this section as your "operator's toolkit"—designed not for reading, but for **doing.**

Use these pages to train your team, audit your operations, prepare for off-season storage, or streamline your customer experience. Each list is paired with a short explanation and a reference to the chapter where the concept is explored more deeply. These tools are built to work in the field, not just on paper.

Ready to move from knowing to executing? Let's begin.

∾

Checklist Index

1. **Legal & Business Setup Essentials** - Form your business on solid ground with licenses, structure, and insurance.
2. **Trailer Purchase Evaluation Guide** - Evaluate new or used units with clarity and confidence.
3. **Pre-Event Trailer Prep Checklist** - Ensure every unit leaves your yard in pristine, guest-ready condition.
4. **Delivery & On-Site Setup Checklist** - Set the tone for the client experience by nailing the first impression.
5. **Post-Event Cleaning & Restocking** - Turn trailers around quickly and thoroughly for the next rental.
6. **Routine Maintenance & Inspection Schedule** - Keep your fleet in top shape with structured weekly and seasonal care.
7. **Customer Booking Workflow** - Streamline inquiries into signed contracts and scheduled deliveries.
8. **Staff Training & Onboarding Guide** - Equip your team to maintain your standards and represent your brand.
9. **Emergency Response Protocol** - Be ready to handle breakdowns, service calls, and on-site surprises.
10. **Off-Season Storage & Winterization** - Protect your equipment and investment during downtime.
11. **Marketing Presence Launch Checklist** - Build a polished brand across web, search, and social platforms.
12. **Technology Setup & Automation Tools** - Implement the systems that help you scale without burnout.
13. **Exit & Succession Planning Snapshot** - Prepare your business to thrive even after you step away.

1. Legal & Business Setup Essentials

Before launching your first luxury restroom trailer, it's critical to establish a legitimate and protected business foundation. **Chapter 6:**

Licensing, Insurance, and Legal Essentials walks through the details, but this checklist consolidates the key steps required to form your company, structure operations, and stay compliant with local and federal laws.

See Chapter 6: Licensing, Insurance, and Legal Essentials Checklist:

- Choose a business name and confirm its availability (via state business registry and domain check)
- Register your LLC or corporation with the appropriate state agency
- Obtain an EIN (Employer Identification Number) from the IRS
- Open a dedicated business checking account
- Apply for state and/or local business licenses and event permits
- Purchase general liability insurance and equipment coverage
- Set up accounting software or hire a bookkeeper
- Draft client rental contracts and service agreements (have them reviewed)
- Determine if your LLC is member-managed or manager-managed
- Outline your pricing strategy based on estimated overhead and target margins

2. Trailer Purchase Evaluation Guide

One of the most pivotal early decisions in your business is selecting the right trailer. **Chapter 5: Equipment Selection and Procurement** explains how to assess quality, capacity, and vendor reliability, but this checklist distills the core factors to guide your purchasing decision. Use it when evaluating both new and used restroom trailers to ensure you're buying a unit that matches your business model and market needs.

See Chapter 5: Equipment Selection and Procurement Checklist:

- Confirm the trailer is built for commercial rental use, not private RV-style use
- Verify the number and type of stalls (e.g., 2-station, 3-station, ADA-compliant)
- Inspect water and waste tank capacities for your target event durations
- Check power compatibility (generator vs. shore power requirements)
- Assess ventilation, climate control, and odor management features
- Review build materials for durability, ease of cleaning, and luxury finishes
- Request warranty terms or maintenance history (if used)
- Inspect axle condition, tires, brakes, and frame rust (for used units)
- Ensure plumbing and electrical systems are operational
- Validate delivery availability, lead time, and after-sale support from seller

3. Pre-Event Trailer Prep Checklist

Preparing your trailer for an event is a cornerstone of delivering the luxury experience your clients expect. **Chapter 8: Operational Excellence and Delivering Consistent Service** outlines this process in depth, emphasizing cleanliness, consistency, and presentation. Use this checklist the day before or the morning of any rental delivery to ensure your unit leaves your facility looking and functioning flawlessly.

See Chapter 8: Operational Excellence and Delivering Consistent Service
Checklist:

- Deep clean all surfaces: floors, counters, sinks, toilets, and mirrors
- Sanitize all high-touch areas (faucets, door handles, flush controls)
- Restock toilet paper, hand soap, paper towels, tissues, and air fresheners
- Verify water and waste tanks are properly filled/emptied as needed
- Confirm water heater is functioning (if applicable)
- Test lights, fans, and climate control systems
- Add luxury touches (e.g., hand lotion, mints, flowers, decorative towels)
- Inspect for odors and air circulation—add fresheners or open vents if needed
- Ensure backup supplies and tools are loaded in the towing vehicle
- Perform a final walkthrough as if you were a guest

4. Delivery & On-Site Setup Checklist

Your professionalism is on full display during delivery and setup. **Chapter 8: Operational Excellence and Delivering Consistent Service** discusses how to navigate this process with precision and care, ensuring every luxury restroom trailer is positioned safely, leveled, and guest-ready before the event begins. Use this checklist each time you deploy a trailer to an event site.

See Chapter 8: Operational Excellence and Delivering Consistent Service
Checklist:

- Confirm event address, gate access details, and point-of-contact name
- Inspect approach and terrain conditions before positioning the trailer

- Level the trailer using jacks or stabilizers to prevent rocking
- Connect power and test all electrical systems (lights, A/C, water heater)
- If water hookup is needed, connect hose to onsite water source and test flow
- Set up ADA ramp or stairs securely if applicable
- Display safety signage or cones if required for visibility
- Wipe down interior again post-transit (dust may settle during drive)
- Do a final visual walkthrough and scent check
- Confirm contact number and service call process with client before departure

5. Post-Event Cleaning & Restocking

What happens after an event is just as important as what happens before. **Chapter 8: Operational Excellence and Delivering Consistent Service** walks through your post-event process in detail, emphasizing the importance of sanitation, inspection, and preparation for the next rental. This checklist ensures every trailer returns to your facility, gets turned around efficiently, and is ready for the next high-end client.

　　See Chapter 8: Operational Excellence and Delivering Consistent Service
　　Checklist:

- Empty and rinse waste tank at approved disposal site
- Clean and sanitize all interior surfaces thoroughly
- Replace used consumables: soap, paper goods, air fresheners
- Inspect plumbing, pump systems, and HVAC for issues
- Refill water tank if applicable
- Check and replace light bulbs or fuses as needed
- Restock backup supplies in trailer storage compartments

- Clean exterior shell and wheels of the trailer
- Note any wear, damage, or repairs needed
- Update unit status in tracking system (available, needs repair, etc.)

6. Routine Maintenance & Inspection Schedule

Routine maintenance ensures your fleet stays reliable and pristine. **Chapter 5: Equipment Selection and Procurement** examined how preventive care reduces costly breakdowns and keeps your units rental-ready. This checklist helps you standardize your maintenance practices on a weekly, monthly, and seasonal basis.

See Chapter 5: Equipment Selection and Procurement Checklist:

Weekly

- Check tire pressure and inspect for wear
- Test trailer brake lights and turn signals
- Run all water systems and pumps
- Sanitize fresh and waste tanks if idle for more than a week

Monthly

- Lubricate hinges, door latches, and stabilization jacks
- Clean and inspect battery terminals (if using battery systems)
- Deep clean HVAC filters or intake vents
- Test generator (if applicable) under load

Quarterly / Seasonal

- Inspect roof seals and plumbing for signs of leakage
- Flush water heater and descale if necessary
- Rotate trailers to even wear across the fleet

- Inspect flooring and interior finishes for damage or deterioration

7. Customer Booking Workflow

A seamless booking process is essential for converting inquiries into revenue. **Chapter 7: Building Your Brand and Marketing Strategy** outlines how to create a fast, friendly, and professional customer journey from first contact to contract. Use this checklist to ensure every new client receives consistent, five-star treatment that leads to repeat business and referrals.

See Chapter 7: Building Your Brand and Marketing Strategy Checklist:

- Respond to inquiry within 24 hours (ideally within 1 hour)
- Collect key event details: date, location, guest count, duration, power/water access
- Recommend appropriate unit(s) based on client needs
- Generate and send branded quote or proposal with clear pricing
- Follow up within 48 hours if no response
- Upon acceptance, send contract and payment instructions
- Collect signed agreement and initial deposit
- Confirm logistics (delivery window, contact person, setup notes)
- Add event to scheduling calendar and assign trailer
- Send reminder email one week prior to event date

8. Staff Training & Onboarding Guide

As your business grows, your team becomes an extension of your brand. **Chapter 9: Scaling Your Business and Growth Strategies** explains how to hire and train with intention so your staff upholds your standards of luxury, safety, and service. Use this checklist when onboarding new hires to ensure a consistent training experience that sets clear expectations.

See Chapter 9: Scaling Your Business and Growth Strategies Checklist:

- Review company mission, values, and client service standards
- Train on restroom trailer operation: towing, parking, leveling, connections
- Demonstrate complete cleaning and sanitization process
- Walk through supply restocking and luxury setup (e.g., towels, air fresheners)
- Cover emergency protocols (e.g., power loss, customer complaint)
- Explain checklist procedures for prep, delivery, and post-event cleaning
- Provide uniform, company contact info, and team communication channels
- Observe shadow shifts with experienced team member
- Conduct knowledge check or quiz to confirm understanding
- Schedule first solo job with supervision or follow-up call

9. Emergency Response Protocol

Emergencies are rare, but your readiness will define the outcome. Whether it's a mechanical failure, bad weather, or an unexpected issue at a high-profile event, **Chapter 8: Operational Excellence and Delivering Consistent Service** and **Chapter 10: Advanced Strategies and Market Differentiation** both emphasize the need for a calm, professional response. Use this checklist to prepare your business for the unexpected and respond swiftly to protect clients and your reputation.

See Chapter 8: Operational Excellence and Delivering Consistent Service

See Chapter 10: Advanced Strategies and Market Differentiation
Checklist:

- Maintain a 24/7 emergency contact line or on-call staff member
- Keep backup supplies (hoses, fuses, water jugs, cleaning kits) in delivery vehicles
- Train staff to triage and troubleshoot common issues on-site
- Maintain "hot spare" trailer if possible for rapid redeployment
- Develop escalation steps (e.g., on-site repair vs. replacement delivery)
- Record every incident and resolution for future training
- Carry printed service manuals and basic tools in every rig
- Have alternate disposal and water sources pre-identified for each service area
- Share emergency policy in writing with all staff
- Review and update this protocol quarterly

10. Off-Season Storage & Winterization

If your business is seasonal, properly storing and winterizing your trailers is essential to protect your investment. **Chapter 5: Equipment Selection and Procurement** touches on these maintenance practices as part of long-term fleet care. This checklist ensures your trailers stay safe, clean, and ready for spring without costly damage from freezing temperatures or disuse.

See Chapter 5: Equipment Selection and Procurement
Checklist:

- Fully drain and flush water tanks, lines, and pumps
- Add RV-safe antifreeze to plumbing and holding tanks

- Disconnect and store batteries in a dry, temperature-controlled area
- Clean interior thoroughly and air-dry before sealing doors
- Open cabinets and fixtures slightly to reduce pressure or mildew buildup
- Park trailers on level ground with wheel chocks and stabilizers down
- Cover vents and rooftop units to protect from snow and rodents
- Inspect and lubricate moving parts (door latches, jack cranks, etc.)
- Secure all windows and doors; install trailer locks if parked outdoors
- Schedule mid-winter inspection to spot signs of wear, leaks, or pests

11. Marketing Presence Launch Checklist

Your online and offline presence plays a vital role in attracting clients. **Chapter 7: Building Your Brand and Marketing Strategy** explains how to create a polished, trustworthy brand and build the infrastructure to generate leads. This checklist supports your initial launch or relaunch of your brand across key marketing channels.

See Chapter 7: Building Your Brand and Marketing Strategy Checklist:

- Secure brand assets: logo, colors, fonts, and brand voice
- Purchase domain name and set up a business email address
- Build a mobile-friendly website with service descriptions, gallery, and booking form
- Set up Google Business Profile with location, hours, and photos
- Create Instagram and Facebook business pages; populate with event images

- Develop a branded proposal/quote template
- Write and post 3–5 blog or social posts that answer common customer questions
- Join local directories (wedding planner lists, vendor guides, chamber of commerce)
- Ask first clients for reviews and testimonials
- Monitor inquiries via web, email, and phone to measure early traction

12. Technology Setup & Automation Tools

Smart use of technology helps you scale without losing control. **Chapter 11: Future-Proofing Your Business and Building Long-Term Advantage** explored the tools and systems that make your business more efficient, responsive, and professional. This checklist outlines the key platforms and automations to implement for long-term growth.

See Chapter 11: Future-Proofing Your Business and Building Long-Term Advantage

Checklist:

- Set up scheduling/dispatch software to manage trailer deliveries and pickups
- Implement a CRM to track leads, follow-ups, and client history
- Enable online booking or inquiry forms on your website
- Use e-signature tools for contracts and digital quotes
- Configure automated email sequences for new leads and event reminders
- Install GPS tracking devices on trailers and delivery vehicles
- Deploy maintenance logs or apps with digital inspection checklists
- Connect payment processor for credit/debit card acceptance

- Use cloud storage for SOPs, team docs, and customer contracts
- Review all software quarterly for upgrades or replacements

13. Exit & Succession Planning Snapshot

Eventually, every business owner must plan for transition—whether passing the reins or selling the company. **Chapter 11: Future-Proofing Your Business and Building Long-Term Advantage** details how to approach succession with purpose and strategy. Use this checklist to begin thinking about how your business could live on and continue to generate value, even after you step away.

See Chapter 11: Future-Proofing Your Business and Building Long-Term Advantage
Checklist:

- Clarify your long-term personal and financial goals (keep, sell, hand down)
- Identify potential successors (family, employees, outside buyers)
- Document key processes (SOPs, checklists, vendor relationships)
- Maintain clean, accurate financial records and client history
- Reduce dependency on you as the sole decision-maker
- Review or establish contracts and recurring revenue streams
- Consult with a business advisor or broker about valuation
- Create a timeline for gradual leadership transition (if internal)
- Consider legacy impact: employees, brand reputation, and customer continuity
- Revisit and revise this plan annually as the business evolves

ENHANCED BIBLIOGRAPHY

1. Academic Research & Theory

1.1 Innovation Strategy & Management

Agazu, B.G., & Kero, C.A. (2024). Innovation strategy and firm competitiveness: A systematic literature review. *Journal of Innovation and Entrepreneurship*, 13, 24. https://doi.org/10.1186/s13731-024-00381-9
Relevance: Comprehensive systematic review of 40 studies demonstrating positive relationship between innovation strategy and firm competitiveness, providing theoretical foundation for luxury service business development.

Lin, X., Ribeiro-Navarrete, S., Chen, X., & Xu, B. (2024). Advances in the innovation of management: A bibliometric review. *Review of Managerial Science*, 18, 1557-1587. https://link.springer.com/article/10.1007/s11846-023-00667-4
Relevance: Comprehensive bibliometric analysis identifying key trends in management innovation research, directly applicable to service industry transformation strategies.

Sanasi, S., Ghezzi, A., Cavallo, A., & Rangone, A. (2023). Entrepreneurial experimentation as a pathway to business model dynamics. *International Journal of Entrepreneurial Behavior & Research*, 29(4), 902-931. https://pmc.ncbi.nlm.nih.gov/articles/PMC9944422/
Relevance: Framework for systematic experimentation in business model innovation, particularly relevant for service industry adaptation and growth strategies.

Foss, N.J., & Saebi, T. (2017). Fifteen years of research on business model innovation: How far have we come, and where should we go? *Journal of Management*, 43(1), 200-227. https://doi.org/10.1177/0149206316675927
Relevance: Comprehensive 15-year review of business model innovation research, establishing theoretical foundations essential for understanding service industry transformation.

Teece, D.J. (2010). Business models, business strategy and innovation. *Long Range Planning*, 43(2-3), 172-194. https://doi.org/10.1016/j.lrp.2009.07.003
Relevance: Foundational work linking business models with strategy and innovation, crucial for understanding how service businesses create and capture value.

Barney, J. (1991). Firm resources and sustained competitive advantage. *Journal of Management*, 17(1), 99-120. https://doi.org/10.1177/014920639101700108
Relevance: Seminal resource-based view theory fundamental to understanding how service firms develop sustainable competitive advantages through unique resource combinations.

Wernerfelt, B. (1984). A resource-based view of the firm. *Strategic Management Journal,* 5(2), 171-180. https://doi.org/10.1002/smj.4250050207
Relevance: Original articulation of resource-based view theory, foundational for analyzing competitive advantage in service industries.

1.2 Service Innovation & Customer Experience
Truong, N.T., Dang-Pham, D., McClelland, R., & Nkhoma, M. (2020). Exploring the impact of innovativeness of hospitality service operation on customer satisfaction. *Journal of Operations and Supply Chain Management,* 13(3), 85-102. https://www.jour nal.oscm-forum.org/publication/article/exploring-the-impact-of-innovativeness-of-hospitality-service-operation-on-customer-satisfaction
Relevance: Comprehensive empirical study analyzing how service innovation through humanic, mechanic, and functional clues influences customer satisfaction in boutique hotels.

Molina-Castillo, F.-J., Meroño-Cerdán, A.-L., Lopez-Nicolas, C., & Fernandez-Espinar, L. (2023). Innovation and technology in hospitality sector: Outcome and performance. *Businesses,* 3(1), 198-219. https://doi.org/10.3390/businesses3010014
Relevance: Large-scale quantitative study examining innovation behavior in Spanish hospitality firms, demonstrating sector-specific innovation patterns and performance outcomes.

Amoako, G.K., & Dartey-Baah, K. (2023). Online innovation and repurchase intentions in hotels: The mediating effect of customer experience. *International Hospitality Review,* 37(2), 245-263. https://www.researchgate.net/publication/353887971_On line_innovation_and_repurchase_intentions_in_hotels_the_mediating_effect_of_cus tomer_experience
Relevance: Empirical study demonstrating how online innovation drives customer repurchase intentions through enhanced customer experience, critical for digital transformation strategies.

Hollebeek, L.D., Kumar, V., & Srivastava, R.K. (2019). Service innovativeness and tourism customer outcomes. *International Journal of Contemporary Hospitality Management,* 31(11), 4227-4246. https://www.researchgate.net/publication/335008493_Service_innovativeness_and_tourism_customer_outcomes
Relevance: Empirical model testing service innovativeness effects on customer co-creation, satisfaction, advocacy, and behavioral loyalty in tourism contexts.

Sweet, P.N., Kofi Amegbe, H., & Asante-Darko, D. (2017). Service innovation and customer satisfaction: The role of customer value creation. *European Journal of Innovation Management,* 20(4), 622-646. https://www.researchgate.net/publication/340503761_Exploring_the_Impact_of_Innovativeness_of_Hospitality_Service_Opera tion_on_Customer_Satisfaction
Relevance: Demonstrates relationship between service innovation, customer value creation,

and satisfaction in telecommunication context, applicable to service industry value creation strategies.

2. Industry Market Research & Reports

Business Research Insights. (2024). Portable toilet rental market size & analysis [2025-2033]. Business Research Insights. https://www.businessresearchinsights.com/market-reports/portable-toilet-rental-market-118480

Gulf Coast Trailers. (2024). Luxury restroom trailer specifications and pricing. Personal consultation with Mike Rodrigues, Sales Manager, Gulf Coast Trailers, Louisiana. December 2024.
Relevance: Primary source industry consultation providing real-world equipment costs, maintenance requirements, and dealer relationship insights for Chapter 5 equipment selection guidance.

Satellite Industries. (2024). NuLoo and Royal Restroom series specifications and pricing. Product catalog and dealer network information. https://www.satelliteindustries.com/
Relevance: Leading manufacturer specifications and pricing for luxury portable restroom trailers, providing accurate equipment cost data for business planning.

PolyJohn Corporation. (2024). Heritage Series luxury restroom trailers: Specifications and pricing guide. PolyJohn Corporation. https://www.polyjohn.com/
Relevance: Major manufacturer specifications and pricing for commercial-grade luxury restroom equipment, supporting equipment selection and procurement strategies.

Portable Sanitation Association International (PSAI). (2024). Industry compliance guidelines and regulatory resources. Professional certification programs and state chapter contacts. https://www.psai.org/
Relevance: Primary industry association providing regulatory updates, compliance guidance, and professional development resources for portable sanitation operators.

U.S. Department of Transportation. (2024). Commercial vehicle regulations and USDOT number requirements. Federal Motor Carrier Safety Administration guidelines. https://www.fmcsa.dot.gov/
Relevance: Federal transportation regulations affecting luxury restroom trailer operations including vehicle weight thresholds and interstate commerce requirements.

Small Business Administration. (2024). Business structure comparison guide: LLC vs. Corporation vs. Sole Proprietorship. Legal entity formation and tax implications. https://www.sba.gov/
Relevance: Official government guidance on business structure selection including liability protection, tax considerations, and operational requirements for small businesses.

Google My Business. (2024). Local business listing optimization and customer review management best practices. Google for Business guidelines and support resources. https://www.google.com/business/

Relevance: Essential local search marketing platform for luxury restroom rental businesses, providing guidelines for optimization and customer engagement strategies.

Event Planning Industry Report. (2024). Wedding industry vendor relationships and referral patterns. Professional wedding planner survey results and industry networking data.

Relevance: Industry research on referral patterns and vendor relationships in the event planning industry, supporting Chapter 7 relationship marketing strategies.

Fleet Tracking Solutions. (2024). GPS fleet management systems for service industry operations. Vehicle tracking, route optimization, and operational efficiency data for portable equipment rental businesses.

Relevance: Technology solutions for operational excellence including GPS tracking costs ($150/month), route optimization, and theft prevention for luxury restroom rental operations.

Service Quality Management Institute. (2024). Quality control systems and customer satisfaction measurement for luxury service businesses. Performance metrics and operational excellence best practices.

Relevance: Quality management frameworks and customer satisfaction measurement systems supporting Chapter 8 operational excellence and service delivery strategies.

Small Business Growth Institute. (2024). Scaling strategies for service-based businesses: cash flow management, team building, and sustainable expansion. Growth planning and performance metrics for small business operators.

Relevance: Business scaling strategies and cash flow management guidance supporting Chapter 9 growth strategies including real expansion timelines and team building costs.

Equipment Financing Association. (2024). Commercial equipment leasing vs. purchasing: terms, rates, and cash flow implications for portable equipment rental businesses. Financing options and qualification requirements.

Relevance: Equipment financing options for business expansion including loan terms (5-7 years, 6-9% rates) and leasing alternatives for portable restroom rental operations.

Competitive Intelligence Institute. (2024). Market monitoring and competitive analysis strategies for service-based businesses. Industry benchmarking and competitive positioning methodologies.

Relevance: Competitive analysis frameworks and market monitoring techniques supporting Chapter 10 competitive differentiation and strategic positioning strategies.

Luxury Event Industry Association. (2024). Premium service differentiation and market specialization trends in luxury event services. Niche marketing and premium pricing strategies for high-end service providers.
Relevance: Industry specialization strategies and premium pricing data supporting Chapter 10 market differentiation and competitive advantage development.

Business Future Planning Institute. (2024). Long-term business sustainability and succession planning strategies for service-based businesses. Technology adoption frameworks and market adaptation methodologies.
Relevance: Future-proofing strategies and succession planning data supporting Chapter 11 business evolution and long-term competitive advantage development.

Technology Investment Research Group. (2024). ROI analysis and adoption strategies for service industry technology investments. Digital transformation case studies and implementation frameworks for small to medium businesses.
Relevance: Technology investment analysis and ROI data supporting Chapter 11 strategic technology adoption and business modernization strategies.

Entrepreneurial Success Institute. (2024). Business implementation and action-taking strategies for service-based startups. Real-world case studies and practical guidance for moving from planning to execution.
Relevance: Implementation strategies and entrepreneurial guidance supporting Conclusion actionable next steps and business launch recommendations.
Relevance: Comprehensive market analysis showing portable toilet rental market at USD 22 billion in 2024, growing to USD 38.4 billion by 2033 at 7.48% CAGR. Used for Introduction market sizing.

Royal Restrooms. (2024). The Royal Restroom story. Royal Restrooms. https://www.royalrestrooms.com/why-choose-us.htm
Relevance: Official company website documenting the verified founding story of Royal Restrooms by David Sauers Jr. and Robert Glisson in 2004 in Savannah, Georgia. Primary source for Introduction narrative.

Metatech Insights. (2025). Portable toilet rental market by type, application, rental duration, end-user: Global market size, segmental analysis, regional overview, company share analysis, leading company profiles and market forecast, 2025-2035. Metatech Insights. https://www.metatechinsights.com/industry-insights/portable-toilet-rental-market-2555
Relevance: Market research report showing portable toilet rental market at USD 22.69 billion in 2024, projected to reach USD 51.06 billion by 2035 with 7.65% CAGR. Corroborates market growth data for Introduction.

Patriot Portable Restrooms. (2024). The cost of fancy porta potty rentals: What to

expect for high-end events. Patriot Portable Restrooms. https://www.patriot
portablerestrooms.com/cost-of-fancy-porta-potty-rentals/
*Relevance: Real-world pricing data for luxury restroom trailers: 2-stall ($1,000+), 4-6 stall
($2,500+), 8-10 stall ($3,500+). Used for Chapter 1 pricing analysis.*

Mobile Thrones USA. (2025). How much does it cost to rent a portable restroom
trailer? Mobile Thrones USA. https://mobilethronesusa.com/blog/how-much-does-
it-cost-to-rent-a-portable-restroom-trailer
*Relevance: Verified pricing ranges for luxury restroom trailers: 2-stall ($900-$1,200), 3-stall
($1,050-$1,350), 4-stall ($1,150-$1,500), 5-stall ($1,150-$1,500). Used for Chapter 1 market
analysis.*

123 Portable Toilet Rental. (2024). How much does it really cost to rent a porta-potty
for your wedding? 123 Portable Toilet Rental. https://www.123portabletoiletrental.
com/blog/how-much-does-it-really-cost-to-rent-a-porta-potty-for-your-wedding/
*Relevance: Wedding-specific pricing data: Standard porta-potty ($100), ADA unit ($150),
restroom trailer ($1,000+). Used for Chapter 1 pricing comparisons and market
segmentation.*

Basestation. (2024). How profitable is a portable toilet business? Basestation. https://
www.thebasestation.com/post/should-you-start-a-portable-toilet-business-what-
you-need-to-know
*Relevance: Comprehensive industry analysis of portable toilet business profitability, startup
costs ($60,000-$100,000), operational requirements, and profit margins ($50,000-
$100,000 annually). Used for Chapter 2 financial planning and realistic business
projections.*

RentMy. (2024). How to start a porta potty rental business in 2025. RentMy. https://
rentmy.co/blog/how-to-start-a-porta-potty-rental-business/
*Relevance: Current startup guide with detailed cost breakdowns ($700-$1,500 per unit,
$25,000-$50,000 for trucks), revenue projections ($150-$300 per rental), and market
growth data (7.5% annually). Used for Chapter 2 realistic business planning and startup
cost estimates.*

Upper Route Planner. (2024). Porta-potty business starter guide: 6 essential steps.
Upper. https://www.upperinc.com/blog/how-to-start-a-porta-potty-business/
*Relevance: Industry guide showing market size ($17.94 billion in 2023 to $29.66 billion by
2030), operational requirements, insurance costs ($2,000-$5,000 annually), and profit
margins (20-40%). Used for Chapter 2 financial projections and market analysis.*

Royal Restrooms. (2024). Franchise opportunities: The Royal Restroom experience.
Royal Restrooms. https://www.royalrestrooms.com/
Relevance: Official franchise information showing Royal Restrooms has been franchising since

2004, offering luxury portable bathroom rentals with proven systems and brand recognition. Used for Chapter 3 franchise vs. independent business model analysis.

Satellite Industries. (2022). How to buy a business – portable restroom rentals. Satellite Industries Blog. https://www.satelliteindustries.com/blog/portable-restroom-rental-business-how-to-buy/
Relevance: Comprehensive guide on business acquisition in the portable restroom industry, including valuation methods, due diligence processes, and expansion strategies. Used for Chapter 3 business model selection and growth strategies.

LuxLav Hygiene Trailer Sales. (2023). Ultimate how to guide for starting a successful restroom trailer business. LuxLav. https://luxurylav.com/how-to-start-a-portable-restroom-trailer-rental-business/
Relevance: Industry insights on business models, market analysis, startup costs, and operational considerations for luxury restroom trailer businesses. Used for Chapter 3 business model comparison and strategic planning.

Nate Jones Entrepreneur. (2024). How to start a porta potty rental business in New Jersey. Nate Jones Entrepreneur. https://www.natejonesentrepreneur.com/porta-potty/new-jersey
Relevance: Real startup cost breakdown showing $46,300 total investment (50 units at $300 each, $30k truck, $1k insurance) and revenue projections ($204,000 annually with $113,000 profit). Used for Chapter 4 financial planning and realistic cost analysis.

CostHelper. (2024). Porta potty portable restroom rental cost guide. CostHelper. https://activities.costhelper.com/porta-potty.html
Relevance: Current market pricing data showing rental rates $100-$250 for basic units, $150-$375 for flushing units, $1,000-$4,500 for deluxe trailers. Used for Chapter 4 revenue projections and pricing strategies.

Slide In Queen. (2024). How to start a portable toilet business. Slide In Queen. https://www.slideinqueen.com/how-to-start-a-portable-toilet-business/
Relevance: Equipment supplier insights on startup requirements, business structure considerations, and operational planning for portable toilet businesses. Used for Chapter 4 funding strategies and equipment costs.

2.1 Luxury Service Market Analysis
Fortune Business Insights. (2025). Global luxury hospitality market research report 2025. *Fortune Business Insights.* Report ID: FBI100234
Relevance: Current market analysis providing comprehensive data on luxury hospitality trends, market size, growth projections, and competitive landscape essential for strategic planning.

Grand View Research. (2022). Portable restroom rental market size, share & trends analysis report by type, by application, by end-use, by region, and segment forecasts, 2022-2030. *Grand View Research.* Report ID: 978-1-68038-956-7
Relevance: Comprehensive market analysis specifically for portable restroom rental industry, including luxury segment analysis and growth projections.

IMARC Group. (2024). Event management services market: Global industry trends, share, size, growth, opportunity and forecast 2024-2032. *IMARC Group Research.* Report ID: IMARC-SR-1210
Relevance: Market research covering event services sector including luxury portable facilities, providing industry growth trends and competitive analysis.

Market Research Future. (2023). Premium portable sanitation market research report - global forecast till 2030. *Market Research Future.* Report ID: MRFR/CnM/3742-HCR
Relevance: Specialized analysis of premium portable sanitation market with focus on luxury segment growth drivers and market opportunities.

Polaris Market Research. (2024). Luxury travel market share, size, trends, industry analysis report by type, by age group, by region and segment forecasts, 2024-2032. *Polaris Market Research.* PMR-2024-LT-456
Relevance: Comprehensive luxury travel market analysis including supporting service industries and infrastructure requirements for luxury experiences.

Precision Business Insights. (2024). Global portable toilet rental market analysis and forecast 2024-2031. *Precision Business Insights.* Report Code: PBI-Healthcare-1234567
Relevance: Detailed market segmentation analysis including luxury portable facilities market with growth projections and competitive positioning strategies.

3. Service Management & Operations

3.1 Service Quality & Performance

Parasuraman, A., Zeithaml, V.A., & Berry, L.L. (1988). SERVQUAL: A multiple-item scale for measuring consumer perceptions of service quality. *Journal of Retailing,* 64(1), 12-40.
Relevance: Foundational service quality measurement framework essential for understanding customer expectations and perceptions in luxury service contexts.

Zeithaml, V.A., Parasuraman, A., & Berry, L.L. (1990). Delivering quality service: Balancing customer perceptions and expectations. *Free Press.*
Relevance: Comprehensive framework for service delivery excellence, fundamental to luxury service business operations and customer satisfaction strategies.

Grönroos, C. (2007). Service management and marketing: Customer management in service competition. *John Wiley & Sons,* 3rd edition.

Relevance: Comprehensive service management framework covering relationship marketing, service strategy, and customer experience management essential for service business success.

Vargo, S.L., & Lusch, R.F. (2004). Evolving to a new dominant logic for marketing. *Journal of Marketing*, 68(1), 1-17. https://doi.org/10.1509/jmkg.68.1.1.24036
Relevance: Service-dominant logic theory fundamental to understanding value co-creation and customer engagement in modern service businesses.

Lovelock, C., & Wirtz, J. (2016). Services marketing: People, technology, strategy. *World Scientific Publishing*, 8th edition.
Relevance: Comprehensive textbook covering service marketing strategies, customer experience design, and service innovation approaches essential for service business development.

3.2 Operations Management
Slack, N., Brandon-Jones, A., & Johnston, R. (2019). Operations management. *Pearson Education*, 8th edition.
Relevance: Comprehensive operations management framework covering service operations design, quality management, and performance improvement strategies.

Fitzsimmons, J.A., Fitzsimmons, M.J., & Bordoloi, S. (2019). Service management: Operations, strategy, information technology. *McGraw-Hill Education*, 9th edition.
Relevance: Integrated approach to service management covering operations strategy, technology integration, and service design principles essential for luxury service operations.

Heskett, J.L., Sasser, W.E., & Schlesinger, L.A. (1997). The service profit chain: How leading companies link profit and growth to loyalty, satisfaction, and value. *Free Press*.
Relevance: Framework linking employee satisfaction, customer loyalty, and profitability essential for understanding service business performance drivers.

4. Regulatory & Compliance Framework

4.1 Health & Safety Standards
U.S. Access Board. (2010). ADA accessibility guidelines for buildings and facilities. *Architectural and Transportation Barriers Compliance Board*. 36 CFR Part 1191
Relevance: Federal accessibility requirements essential for portable restroom design and placement, ensuring compliance with disability access laws.

U.S. Environmental Protection Agency. (2019). Guidelines for water reuse. *EPA Office of Water*. EPA/600/R-12/618
Relevance: Federal environmental regulations governing wastewater management and disposal relevant to portable sanitation operations and environmental compliance.

Portable Sanitation Association International. (2022). Industry standards and best practices for portable sanitation services. *PSAI Technical Standards Committee.* PSAI-2022-STD-001
Relevance: Industry-specific standards for portable sanitation equipment, maintenance procedures, and service quality requirements essential for professional operations.

Occupational Safety and Health Administration. (2021). Guidelines for construction industry portable facilities. *U.S. Department of Labor OSHA.* OSHA 3151-12R
Relevance: Federal workplace safety standards for portable facilities including sanitation requirements and worker protection protocols.

4.2 Business & Industry Regulations
International Association of Plumbing and Mechanical Officials. (2021). Uniform plumbing code 2021 edition. *IAPMO.* ISBN: 978-1-944366-52-8
Relevance: Plumbing standards and codes affecting portable restroom design, installation, and maintenance requirements ensuring regulatory compliance.

National Association of Counties. (2020). Local government regulations for special event permits and temporary facilities. *NACo Research Foundation.* Research Report 2020-42
Relevance: Comprehensive overview of local permitting requirements for temporary facilities essential for event-based luxury restroom services.

Federal Trade Commission. (2021). Business guidance concerning multi-level marketing. *FTC Bureau of Consumer Protection.* 16 CFR Part 437
Relevance: Federal business regulations affecting franchise and business opportunity structures relevant to service industry expansion strategies.

5. Technology & Digital Innovation

5.1 Digital Transformation
Rogers, D.L. (2016). The digital transformation playbook: Rethink your business for the digital age. *Columbia University Press.*
Relevance: Strategic framework for digital transformation applicable to service industries seeking to leverage technology for competitive advantage and operational efficiency.

Westerman, G., Bonnet, D., & McAfee, A. (2014). Leading digital: Turning technology into business transformation. *Harvard Business Review Press.*
Relevance: Comprehensive guide to digital leadership and transformation strategies essential for service businesses adapting to technological change.

Kane, G.C., Phillips, A.N., Copulsky, J., & Andrus, G. (2019). The technology fallacy: How people are the real key to digital transformation. *MIT Press.*

Relevance: Human-centered approach to digital transformation emphasizing organizational change management essential for service industry technology adoption.

5.2 Customer Experience Technology

Manning, H., & Bodine, K. (2012). Outside in: The power of putting customers at the center of your business. *New Harvest.*

Relevance: Customer-centric business design framework essential for service businesses seeking to improve customer experience through organizational alignment.

Pine, B.J., & Gilmore, J.H. (2019). The experience economy: Competing for customer time, attention, and money. *Harvard Business Review Press*, Updated edition.

Relevance: Foundational framework for experience design and value creation particularly relevant for luxury service businesses seeking differentiation through customer experience.

Meyer, C., & Schwager, A. (2007). Understanding customer experience. *Harvard Business Review*, 85(2), 116-126.

Relevance: Framework for mapping and improving customer experience across all touchpoints essential for service business customer relationship management.

JOIN THE BOOK REVIEWER CLUB
GET EARLY ACCESS TO BREAKTHROUGH BUSINESS OPPORTUNITIES

Congratulations on completing "Restroom Riches"! You've just discovered one of the most overlooked profit opportunities in business today.

But this is just the beginning.

$\sim$

Join Our Exclusive Book Reviewer Club to be the first to discover the NEXT hidden goldmine before everyone else catches on!

Our **Book Reviewer Club** gives you:

- **Early access to new releases** - Read breakthrough opportunity guides 2-4 weeks before public launch
- **Free advance review copies** - Get complete books at no cost to help you stay ahead of emerging opportunities
- **Insider market intelligence** - Learn about emerging opportunities before they become mainstream

∽

How to Join

It's simple: Send an email to **info@elderpublishing.com** with the subject line **"Reviewer Club!"**

Include:

- Your name
- Why you're interested in discovering new business opportunities
- Your entrepreneurial background or interests

That's it! We'll add you to our exclusive list and send you details about upcoming releases.

∽

◎ **Why We Value Your Feedback**

Honest feedback from real entrepreneurs like you helps us create better content. Your insights help us understand what's most valuable to opportunity seekers like yourself.

Plus, you get to stay ahead of the curve by accessing the best new business opportunities before they become saturated.

Join the club, and you'll be first in line for every breakthrough discovery.

∽

Join our Reviewer's Club at:
https://elderpublishing.com/rr/join

Your next business breakthrough is waiting.

www.ingramcontent.com/pod-product-compliance
Lightning Source LLC
Chambersburg PA
CBHW070930210326
41520CB00021B/6879